COMPASSIONATE STRATEGIES FOR ANXIOUS ATTACHMENT RECOVERY

OVERCOME ABANDONMENT FEARS AND RESTORE YOUR CONFIDENCE TO BUILD LASTING, SECURE RELATIONSHIPS

ANNE MOIGIS, MA, LPC

HAFIZ

Even after all this time, the sun never says to the earth, 'You owe me.' Look what happens with a love like that. It lights the whole sky.

Thank you for your purchase!

Please scan the QR code below to claim the Bonus Companion Workbook!

Contents

Introduction

E very day, countless individuals navigate the turbulent waters of relationships with a hidden burden that often goes unrecognized even by
themselves—anxious attachment. You might know this experience too well: the
constant worry about being left, the hyper-vigilance about your partner's moods
and actions, and that deep-seated fear that you are somehow not enough. This
isn't just an occasional concern; it's a recurring theme that can dominate your
thoughts and actions, making your relationship feel like a tightrope walk.

This book is your guide to understanding and transforming these fears.
Compassionate Strategies for Anxious Attachment Recovery is designed to help
you overcome abandonment fears and restore confidence, enabling you to build
lasting and secure relationships. My goal is to provide you with a deeper understanding of anxious attachment and equip you with practical, effective strategies
that can lead you toward a more secure way of connecting with others.

Structured to facilitate your healing journey, this book unfolds in a series
of focused sections. Initially, we'll explore the roots of anxious attachment and
its connection to trauma, recognizing that traumatic experiences don't have to
be monumental to have a profound impact. Subsequent sections will offer you
a variety of therapeutic approaches, emphasizing the power of Eye Movement
Desensitization and Reprocessing (EMDR), a therapy I specialize in, which has
shown remarkable success in addressing issues like yours.

I am Anne Moigis, an EMDR Certified Therapist with a background in
trauma and mindfulness techniques. My years of private practice have allowed
me to work closely with many individuals who struggle with anxious attach-

ment, and these experiences have deeply informed the approaches and insights shared in this book.

To you, the reader: I understand the courage it takes to confront these patterns. Your feelings are valid, and your experiences are real. It's important to acknowledge the pain without judgment and to recognize the strength it takes to seek change. This book is crafted to resonate with your experiences, offering empathy, understanding, and actionable steps toward healing.

What sets this book apart is its dual focus. While we delve into the emotional and psychological underpinnings of anxious attachment, we also prioritize practical recovery strategies. This is about more than understanding—it's about action and transformation. Including various therapeutic options, particularly EMDR, provides a comprehensive approach tailored to diverse needs and circumstances.

As we embark on this journey together, remember that each step forward moves you closer to a more secure and confident you. This book is a resource and a companion in your journey to build secure, fulfilling relationships. Let's take this step together, with compassion as our guide and transformation as our goal.

Chapter 1

Foundations of Anxious Attachment

The term "anxious attachment" might evoke a vivid image for those familiar with the relentless worry of whether their loved ones will stay or leave. It may be that moment when you're waiting for a text message that takes forever, each passing minute amplifying your inner turmoil. This isn't just about being "clingy" or "needy," as society too quickly labels it. It's a deeply rooted emotional response that affects your relationships and overall well-being. This chapter will explore the foundation of anxious attachment, understanding its origins, how it manifests in daily life and relationships, and how you can identify its signs.

1.1 The Anatomy of Anxious Attachment: Decoding the Signs

Signs and Symptoms

Anxious attachment often manifests through a spectrum of behaviors and emotions that are reactions to deeply ingrained fears of abandonment and rejection. You might constantly seek reassurance from your partner or friends, needing frequent affirmations of their affection and intentions. This might look like repeatedly checking your phone for messages, needing constant contact, or becoming disproportionately upset over minor delays or changes in plans.

Emotionally, this attachment can feel like riding a perpetual roller coaster. This ride includes intense happiness when receiving affection, then plummeting into worry or despair when you perceive slight withdrawal. These behaviors and feelings aren't choices but rather automatic responses that your emotional brain has learned in an attempt to secure love and care.

Understanding the Origins

The roots of anxious attachment are often traced back to early interactions with caregivers. If, as a child, your emotional needs were inconsistently met—sometimes nurtured, sometimes ignored—you might have developed a hypersensitivity to relational cues as a survival mechanism. This inconsistency leaves a lasting imprint, forming an internal blueprint that suggests that constant vigilance and adaptiveness to others' moods and actions are necessary to secure love and attention.

These early experiences set a pattern that feels impossible to break; they influence how you perceive love and safety, often equating constant attention with care and sporadic attention with the threat of abandonment. Many times in my practice, I have encountered people who are reluctant to look for these patterns with parents. I have had clients who have felt as if they are being disloyal by talking about this history. It is important to remember that understanding this origin is pivotal. It's not about assigning blame or creating conflict. The purpose is to recognize a pattern that began as a means of emotional survival.

Impact on Relationships

Recognizing how anxious attachment affects relationships can be both painful and enlightening. This attachment style can lead to cycles of clinginess followed by withdrawal—a push-pull dynamic where you seek closeness but then feel overwhelmed by fear and pull away. This can be confusing and exhausting for you and your partner, often leading to a turbulent relationship dynamic.

Fear of abandonment can drive you to act in ways that, ironically, might push people away, thus fulfilling your worst fears. This self-protective measure backfires, reinforcing the very abandonment you strive to prevent. This understanding is crucial, and it's the first step towards interrupting these cycles and fostering healthier, more stable relationships.

Self-Reflection Questions

Self-reflection is a vital tool for beginning to untangle the threads of anxious attachment. As a starting point, consider these questions:

1. Reassurance Seeking: How often do you find yourself seeking reassurance in relationships? What specific reassurances do you look for?

2. Response to Conflict: How do you react when a partner or friend pulls away? Can you identify specific emotions and behaviors you exhibit during these times?

3. Self-Worth: How much of your self-worth is tied to how others perceive you or the stability of your relationships?

4. Understanding Needs: Can you identify what you are really asking for when you seek reassurance? Is it love, attention, validation, or something else?

Engaging with these questions is about more than finding immediate solutions; it is about starting a dialogue with yourself. This process can illuminate patterns you weren't fully aware of, laying a foundational understanding essential for the healing process ahead.

1.2 From Childhood to Adulthood: Tracing the Roots of Anxiety in Attachment

The roots of anxious attachment often begin to form in the earliest years of our lives, when the world is understood through the lens of our relationships with our primary caregivers. Imagine a young child whose mother's presence epitomizes warmth and security. When the mother is consistent and predictable in her caregiving, the child learns that the world is a safe place and that they are worthy of love and care. Conversely, when a caregiver's presence and attentiveness fluctuate unpredictably—warm and nurturing one moment, distant or dismissive the next—the seeds of anxious attachment are sown. In these situations, children learn to associate love with uncertainty. They grow up never quite sure what it takes to keep their caregivers engaged, leading to a heightened sensitivity to the emotional availability of others.

This inconsistency can stem from numerous factors in a caregiver's life, including unresolved attachment issues, mental health struggles, or external stresses that divert their emotional resources. The child, unable to understand these complexities, perceives these inconsistencies as a direct reflection of their worth and lovability. The internal dialogue might sound like: "If I can just be good, quiet, or helpful enough, maybe I'll keep their attention." This thought pattern then deeply ingrains the belief that love and attention are conditional and must be constantly earned, setting the stage for anxious attachment to unfold as they grow.

Transition to Adulthood

As children transition into adulthood, their early attachment experiences heavily influence their expectations and behaviors in adult relationships. The strategies they once used to secure love and attention from their caregivers become the strategies they apply to romantic partners or even friends. This might manifest as extreme attention to a partner's moods and actions, an overwhelming fear of being left if they are not perfect, or a continuous search for signs of approval or disapproval. These behaviors often stem from a deeply embedded fear that, without a hyper-vigilant effort, they might once again face the emotional abandonment they experienced as children.

Adult relationships, which naturally involve moments of closeness and distance as people navigate life's ebbs and flows, can thus become a source of significant anxiety for someone with an anxious attachment style. A partner's casual remark or a day spent busy with other tasks might be misinterpreted as an indication of dwindling affection. This misinterpretation can lead to reactive behaviors that can strain a relationship, perpetuating a cycle of fear and misunderstanding that confirms their worst fears despite their partner's best intentions.

Psychological Framework

Attachment theory offers a valuable framework for understanding these dynamics further. Developed by psychiatrist John Bowlby and expanded on by psychologist Mary Ainsworth in the mid-twentieth century, attachment theory proposes that the nature of our early relationships with caregivers influences our understanding of love and security and fundamentally shapes how we connect with others throughout life. This theory categorizes attachment into several styles: secure, anxious, avoidant, and disorganized, each resulting from different early interactions with caregivers. In this book, we focus on the anxious attachment style and pathways to secure attachment.

Breaking the Cycle

Breaking free from the cycle of anxious attachment involves a gradual but intentional process of relearning emotional responses and developing healthier relationship dynamics. This transformation typically starts with gaining an awareness of your anxious attachment style and its origins—a process that might require revisiting painful or confusing experiences from your past. Mindfulness practices can be particularly effective in this regard, helping to ground your reactions in the present rather than old fears and scripts.

Therapeutic relationships also play a critical role in healing from anxious attachment. Therapy offers a safe and stable relational space to explore vulnerabilities and learn new ways of relating based on current realities rather than past fears. Over time, these new experiences in therapy and mindful practices can help rewire emotional responses, making security the foundation of relationships rather than anxiety. Additionally, developing a compassionate self-dialogue is vital. Replacing critical or fearful internal messages with kinder, more reassuring ones alters the internal narrative, paving the way for relationships where closeness is based on choice and joy instead of fear and necessity.

As you progress, remember that each small step in understanding and addressing your anxious attachment style is a move toward a life where relationships are sources of strength and nourishment rather than anxiety and fear.

1.3 The Brain on Attachment: Neurological Insights into Anxious Behaviors

Neurological Patterns

Our brains, intricate and profoundly complex, play a valuable role in how we form and maintain attachments, reacting not just to the present but often to the shadows of the past. When exploring anxious attachment, it's essential to understand the brain chemistry and neural pathways that underpin this condition. What's vital to this is the fight or flight response: a primitive mechanism that prepares your body to either face danger head-on or flee from it. For those with anxious attachment, this response can be triggered not by physical threats but by emotional cues that signal potential abandonment or rejection. This might manifest when a text message goes unanswered longer than expected or a partner seems preoccupied. Sensing danger, your brain floods your body with stress hormones like cortisol and adrenaline, heightening your alertness. Your heart may race, your breathing may quicken, and your muscles might tense, all because your brain is preparing to deal with a threat. Over time, if these responses are triggered frequently—by actual or perceived threats of loss or rejection—they can become the default setting in your neural pathways, making anxious responses more likely and intense.

Attachment and the Brain

Understanding the functioning of the brain's attachment system offers more profound insights into these responses. This system, heavily influenced by early experiences with caregivers, is governed by structures in the brain like the amygdala, hippocampus, and prefrontal cortex. The amygdala, often called the brain's alarm system, processes emotional reactions and is exceptionally reactive to fear. In someone with an anxious attachment style, the amygdala can be hypersensitive, perceiving threats in even benign interactions or moments of disconnection. Meanwhile, the hippocampus, which helps store and retrieve memories, often recalls past experiences of loss or fear associated with attachment, coloring present perceptions and interactions. The prefrontal cortex, responsible for regulating emotions and making decisions, typically works to moderate these responses. However, under intense stress or when overwhelmed by emotional memories, its regulatory capacity can be compromised, leading to heightened anxiety and impulsive behaviors. Together, these brain areas interact in complex ways that can make individuals with anxious attachments quick to sense danger and slow to calm down, perpetuating cycles of anxiety as a result.

Impact of Stress on Attachment

Chronic stress and anxiety can significantly reinforce and exacerbate thought and behavior patterns associated with anxious attachment. When you are constantly stressed, your brain reinforces the neural pathways that support quick, often defensive reactions. This process, known as synaptic pruning, is the brain's way of becoming more efficient based on what it regularly experiences. If your experiences frequently involve anxiety and fear related to attachment, your brain becomes exceptionally proficient at recognizing and reacting to these emotions, sometimes to your detriment. This heightened state can make it challenging to engage in reflective, thoughtful responses in relationships, leading to immediate and often less adaptive reactions instead. Consequently, this dynamic can create a self-fulfilling prophecy, where fears of abandonment drive behaviors that may strain or damage relationships, which in turn perpetuates further anxiety and stress.

Pathways to Healing

Despite these challenges, the brain's capacity for change—known as neuro-plasticity—provides a hopeful pathway to healing. Neuroplasticity refers to the brain's ability to reorganize itself by forming new neural connections through-out life. This means the same flexibility that once allowed anxious patterns to become entrenched can also be harnessed to develop new, healthier thought and behavioral patterns. Engaging in consistent therapeutic practices such as mind-fulness, cognitive-behavioral techniques, and EMDR can gradually reshape your brain's responses to attachment-related stimuli. For instance, mindfulness can help increase awareness of your emotional triggers and reduce reactivity by promoting a state of non-judgmental observation and acceptance. Over time, as these new ways of thinking and reacting become more habitual, they can overwrite the old patterns that have perpetuated anxious attachment, leading to more secure and stable ways of connecting with others. This shift doesn't occur overnight; it evolves through persistent effort and practice. Each step forward in this process of rewiring your brain's response to attachment cues is a step towards a more secure and fulfilling relational life, where fear and anxiety no longer hold the reins.

1.4 Anxious vs. Secure Attachment: A Comparative Analysis

Defining Secure Attachment

Imagine being in a relationship where you feel consistently valued, understood, and respected. In such a relationship, you trust that love is not conditional or fleeting but a stable foundation supporting both partners. This is the essence of secure attachment—an emotional bond engenders feelings of safety, trust, and positive self-worth. People with secure attachment styles tend to believe they are worthy of love and capable of receiving it without undue strife. They also trust that their partners are reliable and emotionally available. This trust isn't built overnight but results from continued mutual respect, open communication, and emotional availability. Such relationships provide a safe haven that allows individuals to confidently engage with the world, knowing they have a supportive base to return to.

Secure attachment does not imply a perfect or conflict-free relationship. Instead, it signifies a robust relationship to handle disagreements and tensions without fear of abandonment or retaliation. Securely attached individuals can manage loss and disappointment in ways that build resilience rather than despair. They can request support without feeling excessive anxiety, and at the same time, they can offer support without feeling overburdened. This balance is vital for promoting a mutual give-and-take that supports personal growth and relational harmony.

Contrasting with Anxious Attachment

The differences between secure and anxious attachment become particularly evident in how each style responds to intimacy and conflict. Where secure attachment encourages openness and trust, anxious attachment often breeds insecurity and fear. Anxiously attached individuals might love deeply, but it's a love riddled with fears of loss and abandonment. These fears can lead to behaviors that unintentionally push partners away, such as clinging too tightly or seeking constant reassurance. Such individuals might interpret a partner's need for space as a sign of cooling affection or escalate minor disagreements into significant conflicts out of fear that not fighting for the relationship might mean losing it.

During conflicts, those with an anxious attachment style often struggle with communication. They might react defensively or aggressively, driven by an undercurrent of fear that any discord will lead to rejection or abandonment. This is a sharp contrast to securely attached individuals who typically view conflicts as temporary, solvable, and even as opportunities to understand each other better and strengthen the relationship rather than threats to the relationship's stability.

Benefits of Secure Attachment

Developing a more secure attachment style can profoundly impact your life, influencing everything from your choice of a partner to how you interact in your broader social world. One of the most immediate benefits is the improvement in relationship quality. Secure attachments are characterized by less conflict, more satisfaction, and greater longevity. These relationships support the growth and well-being of both partners, fostering a cycle of positive interactions and deepening mutual respect.

On a personal level, secure attachment significantly enhances self-esteem. Feeling safe in your relationships makes you more likely to feel good about yourself. You understand that being worthy of love isn't contingent on meeting certain conditions or always being agreeable. This can lead to greater emotional stability and resilience, as you're less likely to hinge your self-worth on how others treat you or on the status of your relationships.

Moreover, secure attachment can improve mental and physical health. Stress from tumultuous relationships can take a toll on the mind and the body. In contrast, secure relationships can be a source of strength and comfort, reducing stress and its associated health problems, such as high blood pressure, heart disease, anxiety, and depression.

Path to Security

The transition from an anxious to a secure attachment style is possible, and this book aims to guide you through this process. In the following chapters, we will work on understanding the roots of your attachment style, recognizing how it manifests in your relationships, and learning new, healthier ways to relate to others. This transformation requires patience and persistence, as old patterns are often deeply ingrained. However, through consistent effort and perhaps with the support of therapy, you can rewrite your relationship script.

Building a secure attachment starts with developing self-awareness and self-compassion. This means recognizing your triggers, understanding your needs, and responding to your triggers and your needs in healthy ways rather than reacting out of fear or anxiety. It also involves learning to communicate more effectively—expressing your needs clearly and listening empathetically to others. As you practice these skills, you can gradually experience relationships based on mutual respect and genuine intimacy—a stark contrast to the fear and insecurity you may be accustomed to.

This shift alters your intimate relationships and enhances your overall sense of security and satisfaction with life. Each step towards secure attachment is a step towards a more fulfilling and resilient life, where relationships are a source of joy and strength, not anxiety and uncertainty.

1.5 The Role of Culture in Shaping Attachment Styles

Cultural Influences

The fabric of our attachment styles is woven with threads of cultural norms and values that color our perceptions of love, duty, and independence. In cultures where collectivism reigns, such as many Asian and Hispanic societies, the interdependence between family members is often profound. Here, caregiving goes beyond the nuclear family and includes a broader community, instilling a sense of security and a strong sense of duty that might suppress open emotional expression. In such settings, children may learn to prioritize family needs over personal feelings, which can sometimes lead to an anxious attachment style characterized by a deep fear of upsetting harmony by expressing needs or desires that might be contrary to family expectations.

On the other hand, in more individualistic cultures, often seen in Western countries like the United States and much of Europe, there is a significant emphasis on self-reliance and personal freedom. Here, caregiving might focus more on fostering independence than interdependence. While this can cultivate a secure sense of self-sufficiency, it can also paradoxically, lead to anxious attachments if the emotional availability of caregivers is inconsistent as they encourage early independence. Thus, children might develop a heightened sensitivity to emotional cues, interpreting independence not as freedom but as a subtle signal of abandonment.

Navigating these cultural nuances is crucial because they frame the language of love and connection we learn to speak. For instance, a person raised in a culture that values stoicism and self-sacrifice might view the emotional expressiveness typical of another culture as bewildering or overwhelming, shaping how they interpret and respond to emotional intimacy in relationships.

Cross-Cultural Comparisons

Studies reveal fascinating insights into how these cultural frameworks influence attachment security and anxiety. Research comparing attachment styles in Eastern and Western cultures shows that the prevalence of secure attachment might be higher in Western cultures, which promote open communication and emotional expression. Conversely, anxious attachment styles may be more common in Eastern cultures, where harmony and collective well-being are prioritized. These studies underscore the profound impact of cultural practices on developing attachment styles from a young age.

For example, a study examining Greek and Dutch infants found differences in the levels of secure attachment, likely reflective of the distinct child-rearing practices and family dynamics prevalent in these cultures. Greek families, with a stronger emphasis on close-knit familial structures and interdependence, tended to have children with less secure attachment styles than their Dutch counterparts, who were typically raised in a more independent and emotionally open environment.

Navigating Cultural and Personal Attachment

Understanding the cultural roots of your attachment style is not about assigning blame but recognizing the diverse influences shaping your approach to relationships. It involves a delicate balance of honoring one's cultural heritage while addressing personal needs that may only sometimes align with cultural expectations. This reconciliation can be particularly challenging for individuals from bicultural or multicultural backgrounds or those who migrate and navigate a cultural landscape vastly different from their upbringing.

Acknowledging these cultural factors is crucial in therapy and healing practices. It allows for a more tailored approach that respects and integrates an individual's cultural identity into their healing process. For instance, therapy for someone from a collectivist background might involve exploring ways to express individual needs without feeling that they are betraying family expectations. Conversely, someone from an individualistic culture might benefit from exploring ways to create deeper community connections without feeling they are sacrificing their independence.

Inclusivity in Attachment Theory

The field of attachment theory must continuously adapt to reflect the cultural diversity of those it seeks to understand. This inclusivity is not merely about being politically correct but about the effectiveness and relevance of psychological theories and practices. By integrating cultural perspectives into the study and application of attachment theory, practitioners and theorists can offer more meaningful support and insights to individuals from varied backgrounds.

As we continue to explore and integrate these diverse cultural perspectives, we help create a more comprehensive understanding of human attachment. This endeavor enriches our theoretical knowledge and enhances practical approaches to therapy and healing, making them more accessible and effective for everyone, regardless of their cultural heritage. As we move forward, let us remember that each cultural narrative adds a unique shade to our understanding of attachment, and honoring these differences is vital to fostering a more inclusive and empathetic approach to mental health and relational well-being.

Throughout this chapter, we have explored the origins of anxious attachment, often rooted in early childhood experiences, and its manifestations in everyday behaviors and emotional responses. Recognizing these patterns is not about placing blame but about gaining insight into how deeply ingrained fears of abandonment shape our interactions with others. By engaging in self-reflection and acknowledging these patterns, you can begin to interrupt the cycles of anxiety and develop more stable, fulfilling relationships. The journey to secure attachment involves mindful practices, therapeutic support, and a compassionate self-dialogue, all of which contribute to rewiring the brain's responses to relational cues. Embracing this process allows for relationships based on trust, respect, and mutual growth, ultimately transforming anxious attachment into a source of strength.

Chapter 2

The Trauma Connection

I magine you're walking through a familiar forest, but today, you step on a seemingly harmless twig, and it snaps loudly underfoot, startling you. This simple, everyday occurrence unexpectedly triggers a flood of anxiety and fear disproportionate to the event itself. This reaction can be akin to experiencing the effects of what many know as 'small t' traumas—subtle yet significant emotional experiences that shape our attachment styles and influence our relationships. In this chapter, we will explore how both 'Big T' and 'Little T' traumas weave into the fabric of our emotional lives, often setting the foundation for anxious attachment patterns that can persist into adulthood.

2.1 Big T and Little t Traumas: Understanding Their Impact

Defining Trauma

The term "trauma" is often associated with significant, life-altering events—what professionals refer to as 'Big T' traumas. These include experiences like serious accidents, natural disasters, war, or severe personal violence. Such events undoubtedly have profound impacts on an individual's psychological state and attachment style, often leading to heightened states of anxiety and pervasive fears of loss or abandonment. However, equally impactful can be 'little t' traumas, which might not meet the same severity threshold but deeply affect personal development and emotional well-being. These could include experiences like ongoing emotional abuse, neglect, the sudden loss of a significant relationship, or even the chronic misattunement of a caregiver whose emotional unavailability left indelible marks during formative years.

Both types of trauma can profoundly influence how you form and maintain relationships. 'Big T' traumas might lead to overt symptoms of post-traumatic stress, such as nightmares, flashbacks, or severe anxiety, which can make forming secure emotional attachments challenging. 'Little t' traumas, while less dramatic, can insidiously undermine your sense of security and worth, leading to an anxious attachment style characterized by a chronic need for reassurance and fear of abandonment. Many times in my practice, I have had clients who think that their experiences are not severe enough to qualify as trauma. Trauma is not something that you judge. It is an experience that overwhelms your brain. These overwhelming experiences can be different for everyone. Understanding these distinctions helps in acknowledging the depth and breadth of experiences that qualify as traumatic and recognizing their potential impacts on your attachment style.

Traumas and Attachment

The link between trauma and attachment is both profound and complex. Traumatic experiences, especially in early childhood, can disrupt the development of a secure base from which a child explores the world. In the absence of consistent and comforting responses from caregivers during times of stress, children can develop an ingrained sense of insecurity and anxiety about relationships. This insecurity often persists into adulthood, manifesting as anxious attachment. Adults with this style may find themselves constantly vigilant and sensitive to the emotional availability of their partners, friends, and colleagues, driven by an underlying fear of being abandoned or rejected once again.

Recognizing how specific traumas have influenced your anxious attachment style is crucial for healing. For instance, if you experienced neglect or emotional unavailability from caregivers, you might find yourself excessively seeking validation and affirmation from others, perpetually unsure of your worth and their commitment. Acknowledging this cause-and-effect relationship can be both validating and empowering, shifting your perspective from self-blame to understanding and paving the way for targeted healing strategies.

Recognizing Personal Traumas

Identifying personal traumas involves introspection and, often, courage. It's about looking back at your life's timeline and pinpointing experiences that felt overwhelmingly stressful or hurtful—those moments after which things never felt quite the same. This exercise isn't about dwelling on the past but recognizing its impact on your present, a critical step in healing. As you reflect, consider the overt, unmistakable 'Big T' traumas and the quieter, subtler 'Little T' traumas that might have eroded your sense of security and self-worth over time.

Healing from Trauma: Trauma-Informed Care

Once traumas are recognized, the process of healing begins. Trauma-informed care is an approach that involves understanding, identifying, and responding to the effects of all types of trauma. It emphasizes physical, psychological, and emotional safety for both providers and survivors and helps rebuild a sense of control and empowerment. For those dealing with anxious attachment, trauma-informed care might involve therapies that focus not only on relieving trauma symptoms but also on building new patterns of attachment. Techniques might include:

- Cognitive-behavioral therapy to reshape thought patterns.

- Mindfulness practices to reduce anxiety and increase emotional awareness.

- Attachment theory-based therapies that directly address relationship patterns.

- EMDR Therapy to process overwhelming experiences.

This form of care is predicated on the notion of healing from the inside out—addressing the root causes of anxiety and insecurity to build a more stable and secure relational foundation. By integrating trauma-informed practices into your healing process, you can begin to loosen the grip of past pains on your present experiences, opening up new possibilities for building relationships based on trust, security, and mutual respect rather than fear and dependency. This shift is not just transformative; it is also profoundly liberating, offering a path out of the cycle of anxiety and insecurity that trauma can create.

2.2 The Body's Involvement: Physical Manifestations of Emotional Trauma

The way trauma imprints itself on the body is profound and often surprising. Trauma is not just a psychological phenomenon; it's a physical one as well. When you experience trauma, your body reacts in a multitude of ways—it stores memories in your muscles, alters your hormonal balances, and can even shift how you physically move through the world. This somatic experience of trauma means that sometimes, long after the mind has forgotten or suppressed a traumatic event, the body still remembers. You might find yourself flinching at a particular touch or feeling a knot in your stomach in certain social situations, even if you can't immediately pinpoint why. These physical responses are not random; they are direct communications from your body, holding the keys to unspoken and unresolved traumas.

Understanding the interconnectedness of your emotional and physical health is crucial, particularly within the context of attachment and trauma. The mind and body do not operate independently; they are parts of an interconnected system that reacts to trauma in a unified way. When you feel safe and secure, your body reflects this, with relaxed muscles and a steady heartbeat. Conversely, when you're anxious or fearful, as often experienced with an anxious attachment style, your body is in a constant state of alert, ready to respond to the threat it perceives. This state of hyperarousal can lead to chronic stress, which, over prolonged periods, wears down your body and mind, manifesting as insomnia, digestive issues, muscular tension, or chronic fatigue.

These symptoms are your body's way of signaling that the emotional distress of past traumas has not been fully addressed.

To begin addressing these physical manifestations of trauma, it's essential to integrate somatic experiences into your healing process. Somatic experiencing is a therapeutic approach that focuses on the sensations of the body rather than the content of the trauma itself. It works by gently guiding you to increase awareness of your body's sensations and helping you release pent-up trauma-related energy. For example, a therapist might help you notice how your body tensely reacts when discussing or recalling a traumatic event and then guide you through processes to help release that tension without overwhelming you. This might involve physical movements, deep breathing, or vocal exercises that help to literally 'shake off' the trauma stored in your body.

Incorporating somatic awareness into your daily life is another crucial step in healing the physical scars of trauma. This can be as simple as regularly checking in with your body to notice discomfort or tension. Perhaps each morning, you take a few minutes to scan your body from head to toe, observing any sensations without judgment. Yoga and mindful movement are also powerful practices for fostering somatic awareness. These activities encourage you to move with intention and attentiveness, reconnecting you with the often-ignored messages your body sends. Over time, these practices can help you recognize and respond to your body's needs more effectively, easing the somatic symptoms of trauma and reducing overall anxiety.

By learning to listen to and interpret your body's signals, you can start to understand your trauma responses more clearly. This understanding is a powerful tool, allowing you to address not just the psychological effects of trauma but its physical manifestations as well. Through somatic experiencing and body awareness practices, you can begin to release the traumatic energy stored in your body for too long, paving the way for a more integrated and holistic healing process. As you become more attuned to your body's needs and learn to address them directly, you'll likely find that your mind follows suit, decreasing anxiety and increasing overall well-being.

2.3 Breaking the Cycle: Healing from Parental Attachment Traumas

The emotional landscape of our childhood profoundly influences the adult we become, particularly in how we form and maintain relationships. Often, the roots of our attachment styles can be traced back to our earliest interactions with our parents or primary caregivers. It's not just about the love and care that was or wasn't given; it's also about the unseen burdens of our caregivers' attachment styles and unresolved traumas. These inherited emotional legacies can shape our expectations and behaviors in relationships without us even realizing it. Understanding this transgenerational transmission of attachment can be both enlightening and daunting. It means looking back with a critical eye, yet it's crucial for breaking the cycle of anxious attachment.

Parents, like all individuals, are complex beings with histories of trauma and emotional learning. A parent's own experience of attachment heavily influences their parenting style. For instance, a parent with an unresolved anxious attachment might be overly protective or excessively anxious about their child's well-being. This hyper-vigilance can unintentionally instill a sense of the world being a dangerous place in the child, fostering anxious attachment.

In understanding these influences, it's helpful to cultivate a stance of forgiveness and compassion towards your parents or caregivers. This isn't about excusing or forgetting the hurt caused but about freeing yourself from a cycle of blame that can keep you tethered to the past. Forgiveness here is a tool for emotional liberation, a way to acknowledge the complexities of your parents' human experiences while also recognizing the impact on your life. This understanding can shift your perspective from seeing yourself as a victim of your circumstances to acknowledging your capacity to change your attachment narrative.

The concept of reparenting offers a profound pathway to healing from parental attachment traumas. Reparenting is about giving yourself what you didn't receive from your caregivers. It involves nurturing your inner child, that part of you that still reacts to old wounds with fear or insecurity. This process requires you to step in as the loving, attentive, and reassuring parent your inner child needs. By reparenting, you create opportunities to heal old wounds and develop the secure attachments that were missing in your early life.

To begin the process of reparenting, it's essential to first connect with your inner child. This might involve reflecting on childhood memories and identifying moments of fear, sadness, or loneliness. Recognizing these moments can help you understand the needs that were not met and how they relate to your current attachment behaviors. Journaling can be a particularly effective tool for this exploration. Writing about your childhood experiences from a place of curiosity and kindness allows you to acknowledge and validate your past pains without being overwhelmed.

Once you've established a connection with your inner child, you can integrate reparenting practices into your daily life. One practical strategy is to develop affirmations that directly address your inner child's needs. For instance, if you recognize a pattern of feeling unimportant or overlooked, you might develop affirmations like "I am fine as I am" or "I have value regardless." Repeating affirmations daily can help to internalize these messages of worth and care.

Another reparenting strategy involves setting boundaries that protect your well-being. Often, those with anxious attachment styles struggle with boundaries for fear of upsetting others or being rejected. However, healthy boundaries are a form of self-care—they help define your relationship needs and expectations. Learning to set and maintain boundaries is a way of caring for your inner child by ensuring they are not overwhelmed or disregarded.

Lastly, engaging in self-soothing activities can reinforce security and comfort. This might include practices like mindfulness, where you learn to stay present with your emotions without judgment, or creative activities like drawing or music, which can be soothing and affirming for your inner child. These activities provide immediate comfort and help build enduring feelings of safety and self-worth.

Through these reparenting strategies, you gradually build a secure base from which a healthier attachment style can emerge. This process is not about erasing the past but about transforming your response to it. As you learn to parent yourself with compassion and consistency, you lay the groundwork for more secure and fulfilling relationships, breaking the cycle of anxious attachment for a more emotionally balanced future.

2.4 Relationship Traumas: Navigating the Aftereffects of Betrayal and Loss

The wounds left by betrayal and loss in relationships can be profoundly destabilizing, often shaking the foundations on which your sense of trust and security are built. When someone close to you—a partner, a close friend, or even a family member—breaks your trust or departs from your life unexpectedly, the impact can reverberate deeply, reinforcing or even creating anxious attachment patterns. You might find yourself questioning the sincerity of past interactions and your capacity to judge character and intent in the future. These experiences can trigger a heightened state of vigilance in your relationships, where you constantly look for any sign that might suggest history is about to repeat itself.

The path to healing from betrayal involves confronting many emotions: anger, sadness, disbelief, and sometimes relief. Navigating these feelings is a delicate process that requires patience and self-compassion. One of the first steps toward recovery is acknowledging the pain without judgment. Recognizing that your feelings are valid and that you need time to grieve the loss of trust is crucial. This acknowledgment helps externalize the experience, allowing you to see it as something that happened to you, not as a reflection of your worth or capabilities.

Rebuilding trust—both in yourself and others—is a gradual process. It begins with understanding that the betrayal was not a reflection of your actions or worth but rather a consequence of the other person's decisions and issues. This differentiation is crucial as it helps to remove the self-blame often associated with such experiences. From here, the focus can shift to slowly rebuilding your confidence in your judgment and intuition. One effective strategy is to start with small trusts—placing faith in friends or family members in minor, low-risk situations. As these smaller acts of trust are honored, your confidence can rebuild, supporting a gradual return to a sense of security in relationships.

Additionally, engaging in reflective practices like journaling can be particularly beneficial. Writing about your feelings and experiences helps you process them in a structured way, providing clarity and insight. Over time, these written reflections can become a testament to your healing journey, showing how far you've come.

The process of grieving lost relationships is equally crucial in the healing journey. Grief is the natural response to loss, and its process helps you come to terms with what has happened, allowing you to adjust to a new reality without the relationship that was lost. It's essential to fully experience this grief without rushing through it. Activities like writing letters that you never send or creating rituals to let go of the relationship symbolically can provide outlets for your emotions, facilitating a thorough and healthy grieving process.

These grieving practices release the pain associated with loss and serve as a foundation for future growth. Through grief, you learn about your strengths and vulnerabilities, gaining insights that can inform how you approach relationships moving forward. This learning is vital in forming healthy attachments in the future, as it helps you identify what you truly value and need in relationships and red flags you might have previously overlooked.

Building emotional resilience is vital to coping with the challenges that arise from relationship traumas. Resilience doesn't mean you won't experience difficulty or distress, but it does mean you're equipped with the tools to navigate and recover from these challenges effectively. Developing resilience involves fostering a mindset that views challenges as opportunities for growth rather than obstacles. Techniques such as mindfulness meditation can be instrumental in this regard, as they help you stay grounded in the present moment, reducing the tendency to ruminate on past hurts or future worries.

Another aspect of building resilience is cultivating a supportive social network. Surrounding yourself with compassionate and understanding people can provide a buffer against the loneliness and isolation that often accompany relationship traumas. These supportive relationships offer a space to express your feelings openly and receive reassurance and perspective, which are crucial for healing and growth.

Finally, setting personal goals can also enhance your resilience by giving you a sense of purpose and direction. These goals can be related to various aspects of your life—career, personal growth, hobbies, or relationships—and should reflect what's important to you and what you want to achieve moving forward. Working toward these goals can help shift your focus from what you've lost to what you can still gain and achieve, reinforcing your sense of control and self-efficacy.

Through these strategies, you can not only navigate the aftereffects of betrayal and loss but also emerge stronger, with a clearer understanding of yourself and a renewed sense of trust in your ability to overcome life's challenges. This growth is not marked by the absence of pain but by the ability to move forward despite it, carrying the lessons learned into future relationships and experiences.

2.5 Building Emotional Resilience: Techniques to Overcome Trauma

Emotional resilience might be envisioned as a deeply rooted tree, swaying in the gusts of a storm but not breaking. In the landscape of trauma and anxious attachment, resilience is what allows you to experience emotional challenges without letting them define or debilitate you. It is the ability to rebound from adversity, adapt to challenges, and endure significant stress with a spirit of endurance and eventual recovery. For anyone healing from trauma, cultivating emotional resilience is not just beneficial; it's necessary. It transforms potential breakdowns into breakthroughs and fosters a robustness that supports survival, growth, and thriving.

Resilience is particularly crucial when dealing with the aftermath of trauma and the anxiety of attachment issues, where emotional reactions can be unpredictable and intense. Building resilience in this context means enhancing your capacity to manage stress and bounce back from setbacks. Certain practices and habits can be profoundly effective in nurturing this quality. Mindfulness, for instance, is a powerful tool. It involves maintaining a moment-by-moment awareness of our thoughts, feelings, bodily sensations, and environment. Mindfulness practices help you observe your reactions to triggers without judgment, essential for breaking the cycle of anxious responses. You learn to recognize your feelings of anxiety or fear as they arise, acknowledge them, and let them pass without being overwhelmed or reacting impulsively.

Journaling is another resilience-building practice that provides a safe space to express emotions and reflect on experiences. Regularly putting your thoughts and feelings onto paper can help process those experiences, providing a therapeutic outlet that might reveal patterns or insights previously obscured by your emotional responses. This habit encourages a dialogue with yourself, where you confront fears, celebrate successes, and plan future steps. Such reflective practices bolster resilience by providing clarity and reinforcing your agency and self-efficacy.

Self-care routines also play a crucial role in cultivating resilience. These routines should encompass physical, emotional, and mental health practices that help maintain balance and wellness. This might include regular physical exercise, which can alleviate some of the physical symptoms of anxiety and trauma, such as tension and insomnia. Ensuring enough sleep, eating nutritiously, and engaging in recreational activities that bring joy are all self-care practices that contribute to a resilient frame of mind. They help stabilize your mood, improve your energy levels, and enhance your overall well-being, making you better equipped to handle emotional stressors.

Maintaining and strengthening emotional resilience over time, especially in the face of setbacks or new traumas, requires ongoing commitment and adaptability. One effective long-term strategy is setting clear, attainable goals that align with your values and aspirations. These goals give you a sense of direction and purpose, motivating you to continue developing your resilience. Regularly revisiting and adjusting these goals helps maintain relevance and ensures they align with your growth and changing circumstances.

Another long-term resilience strategy is continued learning and adaptation. This involves staying informed about new coping skills and strategies, remaining open to trying different approaches, and adapting your methods as your needs and circumstances change. It also means recognizing when certain strategies are ineffective and proactively seeking alternatives. This adaptive approach keeps your resilience strategies fresh and effective and reinforces a growth mindset and continuous improvement.

The role of supportive relationships and communities in building resilience cannot be overstressed. Being part of a community provides emotional support, practical help, and a sense of belonging, all of which are invaluable when re-covering from trauma. These relationships offer validation and understanding, reminding you that you are not alone in your struggles. They can also provide different perspectives, helping you see solutions or alternatives you might not have considered. Furthermore, sharing your experiences with trusted individ-uals can reinforce your sense of reality, which is often distorted by trauma. By cultivating solid and supportive relationships, you build a network of allies who can offer support, advice, and encouragement as you navigate the complexities of healing from trauma and building secure attachments.

Lastly, practicing gratitude can profoundly impact your ability to maintain resilience. Regularly acknowledging what you are thankful for shifts your focus from what is lacking or problematic to what is enriching and positive. This shift can significantly alter your perspective, helping you cope with adversities more effectively. Whether through a gratitude journal, daily reflections, or shared expressions of thanks, regularizing gratitude can reinforce your emotional re-silience, providing a buffer against the adverse effects of stress and trauma.

By integrating these practices into your life, you actively contribute to a foundation of resilience that supports recovery from trauma and a life charac-terized by emotional health and fulfilling relationships. This resilience enables you to face life's challenges with confidence and grace, turning potential adver-sities into opportunities for personal growth and deepening connection.

2.6 EMDR Therapy: A Pathway to Healing Attachment Wounds

Eye Movement Desensitization and Reprocessing (EMDR) therapy is a trans-formative approach to mental health treatment, particularly renowned for its effectiveness in treating trauma. Initially developed by Francine Shapiro in

1987, EMDR therapy facilitates the processing of distressing memories and associated emotions that contribute to a range of psychological issues, including anxious attachment. The core of EMDR lies in its unique use of bilateral stimulation—typically through guided eye movements, tactile taps, or auditory tones—which is believed to stimulate the brain's natural information-processing system.

The essence of EMDR therapy hinges on its capacity to help individuals process and integrate traumatic memories that are often 'frozen' in the nervous system. These unprocessed memories may manifest as triggers in your daily life, influencing your emotional reactions and behaviors without conscious awareness. For those grappling with anxious attachment, these triggers often relate to fears of abandonment and rejection, rooted in early relational traumas that haven't been adequately processed. EMDR therapy aims to transform the emotional charge of these memories, enabling you to respond to present circumstances based on current reality rather than past pain.

EMDR and Attachment

The potential of EMDR therapy to heal anxious attachment is profound. By targeting the specific traumatic memories that underlie attachment issues, EMDR facilitates a reprocessing that can lead to significant changes in how you relate to yourself and others. For instance, if your anxious attachment is rooted in early experiences of neglect or inconsistency, the distressing memories of these experiences might lead you to expect similar patterns in your adult relationships. During EMDR sessions, these memories can be reprocessed, potentially reducing their emotional intensity and allowing you to form a more secure attachment style.

This reprocessing not only alters your emotional responses but also enhances your self-perception. It can shift ingrained beliefs about your worthiness of love and care, directly addressing the insecurities that drive anxious attachment. As these core beliefs change, you might be more capable of trusting others and less fearful of abandonment, paving the way for healthier, more stable relationships.

What to Expect from EMDR

An EMDR session is distinct from typical talk therapy. Initially, your therapist will work with you to establish trust and explain the process thoroughly, ensuring you feel safe and informed. The treatment itself includes phases of stabilization and assessment, where you and the therapist identify specific traumatic memories and the negative beliefs associated with them. The active phase involves recalling these memories while engaging in bilateral stimulation, which is the hallmark of EMDR therapy.

You might experience a range of emotions during this process, but the therapist will guide you through these, ensuring the session remains within therapeutic bounds. The goal isn't to relive the pain but to observe it in a controlled, supportive environment, thereby diminishing its impact. Most clients report a significant decrease in emotional distress associated with the memory after one or more EMDR sessions and, over time, an overall reduction in their anxiety and an increase in emotional stability.

Finding an EMDR Therapist

EMDRIA is the original membership organization for EMDR therapists. The EMDRIA directory lists many EMDR therapists and list their specializations making it easier to identify those likely to understand the nuances of anxious attachment. I would recommend finding an EMDR therapist who is certified. EMDR Certification requires additional levels of continuing education and consultation in EMDR beyond the basic training.

Preparing for EMDR therapy involves both practical and emotional considerations. Practically, you might need to schedule sessions at times when you don't have immediate obligations afterward, as EMDR can be emotionally intense. Emotionally, engaging in self-care practices that promote grounding and stability is beneficial, as these can help manage any distress that might arise while processing difficult memories.

In conclusion, EMDR therapy offers a powerful pathway to healing for those afflicted by anxious attachment. It provides a method to process and integrate traumatic memories that influence current attachment behaviors. By addressing these root causes, EMDR alleviates symptoms and fosters more profound, lasting changes in how you relate to others and yourself. As we progress, the journey continues to build upon these foundations, exploring additional strategies to strengthen relationships and enhance personal growth.

Chapter 3

Strategies for Self-Healing

In the quiet moments of reflection, have you ever noticed how certain thoughts about past interactions or worries about future ones have a way of spiraling, pulling your emotions along with them? It's as if your mind is a stage, and these thoughts are actors performing a drama that affects how you feel and react. This is particularly vivid for those experiencing anxious attachment, where the mind often rehearses worst-case scenarios or replays old conversations that stir up feelings of insecurity and fear. What if you could direct your mind to a different kind of performance? One that fosters calm, presence, and stability? This is where the transformative power of mindfulness comes into play, a practice that can be particularly beneficial in managing the whirlwind of thoughts and emotions associated with anxious attachment.

3.1 The Power of Mindfulness in Healing Anxious Attachment

Cultivating Present-Moment Awareness

Mindfulness, the art of being fully present and engaged with the here and now without judgment or distraction, offers a powerful antidote to the anxious mind. For someone grappling with anxious attachment, the mind often dwells in the 'what ifs' of the future or the 'if only' of the past. This can trigger emotional responses that are disproportionate to the actual events occurring in the present moment. By cultivating present-moment awareness, you begin to break this cycle. Mindfulness trains your brain to anchor in the current experience, interrupting anxious thought patterns rooted in past traumas or future fears. It's like putting a stop sign in front of a speeding train of distressing thoughts, slowing it down to a manageable pace, and eventually bringing it to a gentle stop.

Mindfulness Practices

Integrating mindfulness into your daily routine can be manageable. Simple practices like mindful breathing or body scans can be immensely effective. Mindful breathing involves focusing your attention on your breath, the inhale and exhale, noticing when your mind wanders, and gently bringing it back to your breath. This practice helps reduce immediate stress and anxiety and builds your ability to focus and center yourself amidst emotional turmoil. Body scans enhance this by bringing attention to different parts of your body, observing without judgment any sensations of tension or discomfort, which often accompany anxious thoughts. This awareness can then guide you to release tension, promoting relaxation and grounding.

Reducing Reactivity

One of the transformative impacts of regular mindfulness practice is the reduction of emotional reactivity. When you're less reactive, you do not impulsively respond to thoughts or feelings that might have previously triggered a cascade of anxiety and fear. Instead, mindfulness fosters a space between experiencing a feeling or a thought and acting on it. This space allows you to choose responses that align with your needs and values rather than being hijacked by old fears or unhealed wounds. For instance, if your partner is late to call, instead of spiraling into fear of abandonment, you might notice the anxiety, acknowledge it, and then choose to engage in a calming activity while you wait.

Enhancing Self-Awareness

Moreover, mindfulness enhances self-awareness, illuminating patterns in your thoughts and behaviors that you might not have previously recognized. This heightened awareness is crucial in understanding your attachment style and its triggers. With mindful observation, you can notice what specific situations or actions provoke anxiety and insecurity and, more importantly, how you react to these feelings. This insight is invaluable as it provides the groundwork for addressing and transforming these patterns. For example, you might begin to notice that your anxiety peaks during transitions or uncertainties in relationships. Armed with this knowledge, you can prepare and apply mindfulness techniques more effectively, tailoring them to the most vulnerable moments.

In practicing mindfulness, you are essentially retraining your mind to support a more stable and secure way of relating to yourself and others. It's a gentle yet powerful tool that alleviates the symptoms of anxious attachment and fosters a deeper, more compassionate understanding of your emotional landscape. By bringing your mind back to the present, mindfulness liberates you from the chains of past pains and future fears, paving the way for healthier relationships and a more grounded sense of self. As you continue to practice, you might find that what once felt overwhelming now feels manageable and that a calm, centered presence becomes your new baseline, transforming how you relate to others and how you experience the world. Through mindfulness, the stage of your mind can host a more harmonious play where peace and presence are the stars, guiding you toward a life of greater emotional freedom and connection.

3.2 Inner Child Work: Reconnecting and Healing

The concept of the 'inner child' is not merely a poetic metaphor but a psychological reality that plays a significant role in our emotional and relational lives, particularly for those grappling with anxious attachment. This inner child represents the original, instinctual self that experienced the world purely and deeply before being shaped by life's complexities and defenses. It holds our capacity for spontaneous joy, fear, anger, and love. For individuals experiencing anxious attachment, reconnecting with this part of oneself can be profoundly healing. It involves acknowledging and nurturing the parts of you that may have been neglected or traumatized during your formative years.

Engaging in dialogue with your inner child can be a transformative exercise, allowing you to access and heal the root causes of your fears and insecurities. Imagine sitting across from a younger version of yourself, one who might still be hurting or scared. What would you say to them? How would they express their needs and fears? Initiating this dialogue can begin with writing a letter to your inner child. In this letter, express understanding and compassion for their experiences. Validate their feelings and reassure them of their worth. This exercise isn't just about remembering past hurts; it's about actively comforting and providing for that younger self who may not have received the emotional support they needed.

Healing childhood wounds is a delicate process that requires patience and sensitivity. It involves identifying specific experiences that contributed to the development of anxious attachment. This might include moments of feeling abandoned, criticized, or misunderstood. Reflecting on these moments allows you to see their impact on your relationship patterns. For instance, if you were frequently criticized as a child, you might now find that you are overly sensitive to your partner's feedback, interpreting it as a sign of disapproval or rejection. By connecting these dots, you can challenge and change these reactive patterns, replacing them with responses rooted in your current reality rather than your past experiences.

Reparenting yourself is a powerful method to provide the care and validation your inner child was denied. This involves stepping into the role of the parent you needed but perhaps didn't have. It's about affirming your inner child's worth, attending to their emotional needs, and setting boundaries that protect and comfort them. Reparenting looks like setting aside regular time for activities that bring you unconditional joy. These simple pleasures delighted you as a child but were dismissed as frivolous or unimportant. It could also involve creating routines that provide the structure and safety you craved but didn't receive. Simple affirmations can be part of this practice, too—phrases like "I am enough," "I am worthy of love," or "It's okay to feel scared" can be powerful reminders to your inner self of your intrinsic worth.

Through these practices, you heal old wounds and empower your adult self to form healthier, more secure attachments. Engaging with your inner child allows you to retrieve the parts of yourself that may have been lost to trauma and fear. It invites you to reinstate those parts into your current life, not as sources of pain but as sources of strength and authenticity. As you nurture and integrate your inner child, you may find that the fear and anxiety that once seemed an inescapable part of your relationships begin to give way to a more grounded and confident way of connecting with yourself and others. This healing is not a return to a state before trauma but a creation of something new: a state where you can engage with the world and others freely, with your whole self.

3.3 Developing Self-Compassion: A Step-by-Step Guide

In the intricate dance of relationships, especially for those with anxious attachment, the steps can sometimes feel less like a waltz and more like a precarious shuffle. In these moments, the harsh spotlight often turns inward, illuminating every misstep with criticism and self-doubt. This internal critic can be relentless, echoing old messages of unworthiness or fears of abandonment. Yet, imagine transforming that critical voice into one of understanding and support that champions your efforts and soothes your fears. This transformation is at the heart of developing self-compassion, an essential element for healing from anxious attachment. Unlike self-esteem, which is often based on evaluations of worthiness or success, self-compassion doesn't require judging yourself as "good" or "better" than others. It simply asks you to treat yourself with the kindness and understanding you would offer a dear friend.

Cultivating self-compassion begins by recognizing that suffering and imperfection are parts of the human experience that connect us rather than isolate us. When you embrace this viewpoint, the setbacks or struggles you face in your relationships no longer appear as personal failings, but as universal challenges everyone encounters. One practical way to foster self-compassion is through writing letters to yourself. This exercise involves composing letters from a compassionate perspective, addressing a younger version of yourself, or responding to a recent struggle. These letters focus on expressing understanding and encouragement rather than criticism. Use words that soothe and comfort, that acknowledge the pain without amplifying it. For instance, you might write about a recent conflict in a relationship, not to critique your actions but to acknowledge the difficulty of the situation and affirm your efforts to navigate it with integrity.

Another enriching practice is self-kindness meditation, which can profoundly shift your internal dialogue. This form of meditation focuses on generating warmth and compassion towards yourself. You might begin by visualizing someone who loves you unconditionally and imagining the love and warmth they feel for you. Gradually, extend these feelings to yourself, repeating affirmations reinforcing your worth and right to compassion. Phrases like "May I be kind to myself" or "May I accept myself as I am" can be powerful mantras that reshape your self-perception over time.

Overcoming self-criticism is another crucial step in nurturing self-compassion. This often ingrained habit can be remarkably tenacious for those with anxious attachment, where fears of rejection and abandonment can trigger harsh self-judgments. To counter this, start by simply noticing when the critical voice arises. Observe what triggers it, whether it's a perceived mistake or a moment of vulnerability. Recognize this voice as a protective mechanism that once might have served to guard you against emotional pain but is no longer serving your best interests. Then, consciously choose to respond with kindness rather than criticism. This might involve reframing critical thoughts more compassionately or gently reminding yourself that mistakes are learning opportunities, not evidence of inadequacy.

Building a compassionate inner voice is the most transformative aspect of this journey. This voice becomes an internal ally rather than an adversary, offering encouragement and comfort during stress or self-doubt. Developing this voice requires regular practice, much like strengthening a muscle. It involves consistently engaging with yourself in a supportive and understanding manner. When faced with challenges or setbacks, ask yourself what you would say to a friend in the same situation. This perspective can help shift your internal dialogue to be more forgiving and encouraging. Over time, this compassionate voice can become your default response to stress, reducing anxiety and enhancing emotional resilience, fostering healthier and more secure attachments in your relationships.

In embracing self-compassion, you heal old wounds and equip yourself with a profound tool for navigating the complexities of relationships with grace and confidence. By transforming the critical inner voice into one of compassion, you open up a space for genuine self-acceptance and love, laying a foundation for deeper connections with others and a more fulfilling life.

3.4 The Role of Self-Care in Attachment Recovery

In the pursuit of healing and building healthier attachments, self-care extends far beyond the occasional indulgence. It encompasses a broad spectrum of practices that nurture your emotional, physical, and mental well-being. Self-care is fundamentally about fostering an environment where you can thrive, ensuring your needs are met with the same dedication you might offer others. For those recovering from anxious attachment, where there can often be a tendency to prioritize others' needs at the expense of one's own, developing a robust self-care routine is crucial. It's about creating a balance where your needs are recognized and actively fulfilled, providing a stable foundation from which secure attachments can grow.

Self-care can manifest in numerous forms, each serving a unique purpose in your healing process. Physical activities such as yoga, walking, or dance can be incredibly beneficial. They not only improve physical health but also help release the pent-up stress and tension that often accompany anxiety. These activities' rhythmic, repetitive motions provide a physical outlet for emotions, channeling them into movements that heal rather than harm. Simultaneously, these activities encourage the production of endorphins, often referred to as 'feel-good' hormones, which can elevate your mood and provide a natural counter to feelings of depression or anxiety.

On the other end of the spectrum, creative expression—through painting, writing, music, or any other form—offers a powerful means of processing and expressing emotions that might be too complex or overwhelming to articulate verbally. Engaging in creative activities can provide a sense of accomplishment and joy, not necessarily linked to external validation but as a celebration of self-expression. Moreover, creative pursuits can serve as mindfulness practice, focusing your mind on the task and allowing you to escape the cycle of anxious thoughts about past or future attachments.

Social engagement is another critical element of self-care, especially for those dealing with anxious attachment. Isolation can often exacerbate feelings of anxiety and insecurity. By nurturing relationships with friends, family, or support groups, you create a support network that can offer comfort and perspective. These relationships can remind you that you're not alone in your struggles, providing a sense of connection and belonging that is vital for emotional health.

The personalization of self-care is a journey of trial and error. What works wonderfully for one person might not resonate with another, and that's perfectly fine. Exploring different self-care practices is essential to discover what nourishes and supports you. This might mean trying out several activities before you find the ones that help you feel balanced and calm. It's also about recognizing when certain practices must be adjusted or replaced as your needs and circumstances evolve. Keeping a self-care journal can be helpful in this exploration, allowing you to note what you tried, how it made you feel, and whether it's something you want to incorporate into your routine regularly.

Setting boundaries around self-care is equally essential. This involves dedicating specific times and spaces for self-care activities and communicating these boundaries to others. For individuals who tend to prioritize others' needs, setting and maintaining these boundaries can be challenging but necessary. It's about affirming that your needs are important and that taking care of yourself is not a luxury but a necessity. This might look like scheduling regular 'self-care' appointments on your calendar, just as you would any important commitment, and treating these times with the same respect and importance. It could also involve learning to say no or to delegate tasks when your schedule becomes too crowded, ensuring that your commitment to self-care is not the first thing to be sacrificed.

Through dedicated self-care practices, you not only enhance your well-being but also build a stronger, more resilient self that can engage in relationships from a place of strength and fullness rather than neediness or fear. This shift is crucial for anyone recovering from anxious attachment, as it supports the development of healthier, more balanced relationships. As you continue to invest in your self-care, you may find that the anxieties and insecurities that once felt so dominating begin to recede, replaced by a newfound confidence and peace that enriches all areas of your life.

3.5 Building a Self-Soothing Toolkit: Practical Exercises

In moments of distress, where the familiar grip of anxiety tightens around your thoughts and actions, having a personalized toolkit for self-soothing can be your greatest ally. This toolkit is not a physical box but a collection of strategies and practices that you can draw upon to calm your nervous system and regain a sense of control. Developing this toolkit involves a deep understanding of your triggers, those situations, words, or actions that disproportionately ignite feelings of anxiety or fear related to your attachment experiences. Identifying these triggers is the first step toward empowerment, as it allows you to prepare and respond effectively rather than being caught off guard.

When considering your triggers, reflect on moments when your anxiety seems to spike—perhaps it's during periods of uncertainty in a relationship or when communication from a partner is delayed. Start by documenting these instances, noting what was happening, how you felt, and how you reacted. This record becomes a map, highlighting patterns and specific triggers, guiding you to tailor your self-soothing strategies effectively. For instance, if you find that a lack of immediate responses from loved ones triggers anxiety, one of your toolkit strategies might be to write down rational thoughts or affirmations that you can read back to yourself in these moments, reminding you of the many benign reasons a response might be delayed.

With your triggers mapped out, you can explore various self-soothing techniques. Grounding exercises are a cornerstone of emotional regulation, beneficial when you feel overwhelmed by distressing emotions. These exercises focus on reconnecting you with the present moment, often through sensory engagement. A simple yet powerful grounding technique involves the "5-4-3-2-1" exercise, where you identify five things you can see, four things you can touch, three things you can hear, two things you can smell, and one thing you can taste. This method effectively diverts attention from distressing thoughts and anchors your senses in the here and now, providing a break from the intensity of emotional stress.

Sensory engagement can also be tailored to your specific comforts. For example, keeping a small object with a texture that you find soothing, like a smooth stone or a piece of soft fabric, can serve as a tactile anchor, providing immediate comfort when rubbed or held during anxious moments. Similarly, essential oils with calming scents like lavender or chamomile can engage your olfactory senses, promoting relaxation. Integrating these sensory methods into your daily routine can make them more effective, as frequent use reinforces their soothing properties.

Affirmations, too, are a powerful technique in your self-soothing toolkit. These short, positive statements are designed to challenge and undermine the negative beliefs that often fuel anxious attachment reactions. Crafting affirmations addressing your fears and anxieties can provide significant emotional relief. For example, if fear of abandonment is a trigger, an affirmation like "I am whole within myself, and I am worthy of love, whether I am alone or with others" can be a powerful reminder of your intrinsic worth. Repeating this affirmation during times of anxiety can help shift your mindset from one of fear to one of self-assurance and acceptance.

Creating a go-to plan for moments of distress is the next step, emphasizing the importance of preparation and practice. This plan should detail which strategies to use based on different triggers or levels of anxiety. For mild anxiety, a few deep breaths and a reassuring affirmation might suffice. For more intense anxiety, a combination of grounding exercises, sensory engagement, and perhaps a call to a supportive friend could be necessary. Having this plan written down, perhaps in a journal or a digital note on your phone, ensures that it is easily accessible when you need it most.

The effectiveness of your self-soothing toolkit can grow significantly with regular practice and review. Periodically evaluating how well your chosen strategies alleviate your anxiety is crucial. This might involve tweaking or introducing new methods if specific techniques are less effective. The goal is to develop a dynamic set of practices that evolve with your needs, providing reliable support as you navigate the complexities of relationships and personal growth. Through this thoughtful compilation and ongoing adaptation of self-soothing practices, you forge a path toward greater emotional autonomy and resilience, equipped to handle the ebbs and flows of attachment-related anxieties with grace and self-compassion.

3.6 Journaling for Emotional Clarity and Release

Journaling, a practice as simple as it is profound, is a gateway to the innermost chambers of your thoughts and emotions. When you journal, you engage in a dialogue with yourself that can reveal hidden feelings, illuminate patterns, and chart a course through the often turbulent waters of anxious attachment. For many, the blank page becomes a confidant, an unjudging listener that allows for the free expression of thoughts and emotions that might be too complex or daunting to communicate otherwise. This process is precious as it not only aids in processing these emotions but also in clarifying them, transforming a tangled web of feelings into understandable threads that can be addressed and woven into new narratives of self-understanding and healing.

The benefits of journaling are manifold. Primarily, it serves as a tool for emotional clarity. As you write about your experiences, you may find that the very act of putting thoughts on paper helps organize and clarify them, making it easier to understand your emotional triggers and the root causes of your anxiety. This clarity is vital for those dealing with anxious attachment, where emotions can often feel overwhelming or inexplicably intense. Moreover, journaling can track your emotional growth and healing over time. By regularly documenting your thoughts and feelings, you create a record that can be revisited, allowing you to see how patterns have shifted, how far you have come, and what challenges still lie ahead. This record can be incredibly encouraging, providing tangible evidence of your emotional development and resilience.

To deepen your journaling practice, specific prompts can guide your reflections, especially when exploring your attachment style and understanding your relationship behaviors. Consider prompts such as, "What situations make me feel anxious or insecure in my relationships?" or "How do I typically react when I feel ignored or unimportant, and why might that be?" These questions encourage you to probe deeper into your attachment style, helping you uncover the underlying beliefs and experiences that shape your interactions with others. Another powerful prompt might be, "What does a secure attachment look like to me, and what steps can I take to cultivate it?" This helps you envision a goal and sets the stage for planning practical steps toward achieving more secure relationships.

Reflective journaling, a practice that encourages deeper exploration of your inner thoughts and emotional patterns, is another enriching aspect of this journey. This form of journaling goes beyond mere documentation of events or feelings—it involves analyzing them, questioning their origins, and understanding their impact on your life. It's about connecting your current experiences and past events, drawing insights that can inform your path to healing. Reflecting on questions like, "When do I feel most loved and supported?" or "What fears surface in my close relationships, and what might they be telling me about my needs?" can open new avenues for personal insight and emotional growth.

In addition to traditional written journaling, creative journaling techniques such as drawing or collage offer alternative methods for expressing and processing emotions. These visual forms of journaling can be beneficial when words feel inadequate, or emotions are too complex to untangle through writing alone. By creating a visual representation of your feelings, you may discover new layers of emotion or see patterns that weren't apparent before. For instance, you might draw images representing different relationship experiences, using colors and shapes to express feelings that words can't capture. Similarly, creating a collage from magazine images or photographs can be a powerful way to visualize your hopes for future relationships or to represent the journey of healing from past wounds.

These varied journaling practices equip you with a versatile toolkit for emotional expression and self-discovery. Whether through written words, reflective questions, or creative expression, each entry helps you navigate the complexities of anxious attachment, fostering a deeper understanding of yourself and your relational dynamics. This ongoing dialogue with yourself not only aids in processing past traumas and current anxieties but also strengthens your capacity for self-compassion and emotional resilience, paving the way for more secure and fulfilling relationships.

As this chapter closes, remember that each page you fill in documents your journey and contributes to your growth. The insights gained, the emotions processed, and the patterns uncovered all weave together to form a stronger, more self-aware you. As you move forward, let the pages of your journal be both a testament to your challenges and a beacon of your progress, guiding you toward a future where attachment fosters security and joy, not anxiety and fear.

Chapter 4

Forming Secure Attachments

I magine you are in a garden where each flower represents a relationship in your life. As a gardener nurtures each plant to blossom, understanding and fostering secure attachments can allow your relationships to flourish beautifully. Secure attachments are not just romantic concepts but are built on trust, mutual respect, and effective communication. They thrive in an environment where emotional safety allows individuals to express themselves fully and openly. This chapter guides you through the essential components of forming and sustaining secure attachments, helping you turn the garden of your relationships into a vibrant and nurturing space.

4.1 The Ingredients of a Secure Attachment

Characteristics of Securely Attached Relationships

Securely attached relationships are akin to a dance where each partner understands and responds gracefully and with assurance to the other's moves. Trust, mutual respect, and effective communication are at the core of such relationships. Trust allows you to feel safe and confident with your partner, knowing that you can rely on them and that they have your best interests at heart. Mutual respect involves honoring each other's individuality, differences, and boundaries without judgment. Effective communication acts as the rhythm that keeps the dance fluid and synchronized, enabling you to express your thoughts and feelings openly and honestly while being receptive to your partner's.

These relationships are marked by a comforting sense of predictability and reliability but leave room for growth and change. They allow you to be vulnerable, knowing your openness is met with support and understanding, not ridicule or dismissal. In a securely attached relationship, conflicts, though inevitable, are managed in ways that promote understanding and closeness rather than creating distance or resentment.

Assessing Relationship Health

To cultivate a garden, a gardener must first understand the current state of the plants. Similarly, assessing the health of your relationships is a critical step towards nurturing them. Consider how well your relationships meet the criteria of trust, respect, and communication. Do you feel safe and supported? Are your thoughts and feelings valued? Are conflicts resolved in a way that deepens understanding and connection? Reflecting on these questions can help you identify areas of strength that need attention and care.

Cultivating Security in Existing Relationships

Enhancing the security of your existing relationships involves actively nurturing these essential ingredients. Begin by fostering an environment where open communication is encouraged and valued. Share your feelings and needs with your partner, and invite them to do the same. Show appreciation for each other's contributions to the relationship, acknowledging that each of you plays a vital role in its health and longevity.

Furthermore, focus on building mutual support and understanding. Be present and attentive, offering empathy and compassion rather than solutions or judgments when your partner shares their struggles or concerns. This supportive presence tells your partner that they are not alone and that they can count on you, strengthening the trust and bond between you.

Attracting Secure Relationships

Attracting securely attached relationships begins with understanding what you value and need in a partner. Reflect on the important characteristics—trust, respect, empathy, and shared values. Being clear about your expectations helps you navigate relationships more effectively, making recognizing potential partners who share these ideals easier.

Additionally, consider how you present yourself in relationships. Are you open, honest, and respectful? Do you offer the kind of trust and communication you hope to receive? Relationships are mirrors, reflecting what we project and what we are willing to accept. By embodying the qualities of secure attachment, you attract individuals who value and practice those same qualities, paving the way for healthy, supportive, and enduring relationships.

In this chapter, we explore how to recognize and cultivate the kind of relationships that enrich your life and nourish your emotional well-being. Whether you are looking to strengthen your current relationships or seeking new ones, understanding and applying these principles can help you build secure and fulfilling connections. As you turn each page, consider how these insights can be planted like seeds in your relational garden, each holding the promise of growth, beauty, and stability.

4.2 Communicating Needs and Boundaries Effectively

In the tapestry of human relationships, transparent and honest communication is the thread that holds everything together, ensuring each pattern meets the eye with clarity and intention. For those seeking to develop and maintain secure attachments, the ability to communicate effectively is not just beneficial—it's essential. It's about creating an environment where both parties feel understood and valued, where the air is clear of misunderstandings that can cloud connections. Emphasizing clear, honest communication means prioritizing transparency and openness, ensuring that your words match your feelings and intentions. This alignment reduces confusion and builds trust, making it easier for others to relate to and connect with you genuinely.

One of the fundamental aspects of effective communication in relationships is the ability to express your needs clearly. It is crucial to understand and articulate what you need from a relationship, whether it's emotional support, time, or understanding. However, recognizing these needs within yourself can sometimes be challenging, primarily if past experiences have taught you to prioritize others' needs above yours. Start by spending time in introspection; reflect on moments when you felt disappointed or frustrated in your relationships. Often, such emotions are indicators of unmet needs. Once you've identified these needs, practice expressing them to others. Start with more minor, less charged situations to build your confidence. You might say, "I feel valued when we spend uninterrupted time together; can we arrange a regular date night?" Such explicit expressions inform your partner about your needs and invite them to respond, fostering a deeper connection and understanding.

Setting and respecting boundaries is equally critical in cultivating healthy, secure relationships. Boundaries help define where your limits lie and how you wish to be treated by others. They are personal and can vary significantly from one person to another, encompassing physical space, emotional comfort, and mental peace. Setting boundaries might feel daunting if you're worried about how others will respond, but establishing them is a sign of self-respect and self-care. Begin by identifying areas where you feel overwhelmed or uncomfortable in your relationships—these are likely places where boundaries are needed. Communicate these boundaries clearly to your partner without apology, for example, "I need some time to myself each evening to unwind. I would appreciate it if we could respect this space for each other." Remember, setting boundaries is not an act of separation but a clarification that enriches how you engage with each other.

Navigating difficult conversations with empathy and assertiveness is a skill that significantly enhances relationship dynamics. These conversations, whether about conflicting desires, mistakes, or hurt feelings, require a delicate balance of honesty and compassion. Approach these discussions with a clear intention of finding understanding rather than assigning blame. Use "I" statements to express your feelings without making the other person defensive. For example, instead of saying, "You never listen to me," try to say, "I feel unheard when we talk about this topic, and it's important to me that we understand each other." This approach focuses on feelings and needs without accusing or alienating the other person. Additionally, be open to hearing their perspective. This reciprocal understanding can transform a potentially divisive conversation into an opportunity for growth and deeper bonding.

By building your skills in these areas, you enhance your ability to form secure attachments and your overall emotional intelligence. You equip yourself with the tools needed to navigate the complexities of relationships with grace and confidence. As you practice these skills, they become more natural, gradually weaving a more substantial, resilient connectivity fabric in your personal and professional life.

4.3 Navigating Conflict with Compassion and Clarity

Relationship conflict often carries a negative connotation, conjuring images of heated arguments and emotional turmoil. However, when approached with mindfulness and compassion, conflict can become a powerful catalyst for growth and deeper understanding between partners. Rather than viewing conflicts as threats to the stability of a relationship, reframe them as opportunities for strengthening bonds and enhancing mutual understanding. Each disagreement gives you insight into your partner's thoughts and feelings, and, importantly, it reveals your patterns and triggers. This shift in perspective can change how you handle disagreements, turning them into constructive sessions that build rather than erode your relationship's foundation.

The art of compassionate conflict resolution involves addressing disputes with empathy and a genuine intention to understand the other person's point of view. Begin by actively listening to your partner without immediately formulating a response. This type of listening requires you to fully engage with your partner's words, tone, and body language without judgment. The goal here is not to win an argument or defend your stance at all costs but to understand the deeper needs and emotions fueling your partner's reactions. For instance, if a conflict arises from a misunderstanding about spending time together, consider what underlying needs are expressed. Is it necessary for security, attention, or reassurance of their importance in your life?

Once you clearly understand the underlying issues, address these needs directly and thoughtfully. Articulate your perspectives and feelings using "I" statements, such as "I feel neglected when we don't spend much time together, and I need to feel more connected with you." This approach focuses on your feelings and avoids blaming or criticizing the other person, which can escalate tensions. In doing so, you open up a space for honest and constructive dialogue, where solutions are sought that acknowledge and respect each person's needs and boundaries.

Preventing the escalation of conflicts is crucial and can often be achieved by recognizing when emotions are becoming too intense to continue a productive conversation. In these moments, taking a short break can be beneficial. This isn't about avoiding the issue but rather giving both parties the time to cool down and collect their thoughts. Agreeing on a signal in advance, like saying, "I need a moment to calm down," can help implement this strategy effectively. During this time-out, engage in activities that reduce your stress and help you regain a calm state of mind, such as deep breathing, a short walk, or even some physical exercise. When both of you feel more centered and less reactive, reconvene the discussion with renewed focus and a softer heart.

When navigated thoughtfully, conflicts can lead to significant personal growth and a stronger relationship. Each conflict presents a unique opportunity to learn more about each other's desires, fears, and expectations. It allows both partners to practice patience, empathy, and problem-solving skills. Moreover, successfully resolving conflicts can reinforce the trust and commitment between partners, demonstrating a mutual willingness to understand and care for each other's needs. Over time, these experiences build a repository of positive interactions that can help mitigate the impact of future disagreements, ensuring that both partners feel secure and valued in the relationship.

In embracing these practices, you encourage a relationship environment where conflicts are not feared but are seen as natural, manageable, and ultimately beneficial aspects of your shared life. This approach not only deepens your connection but also enriches your journey together with greater understanding and respect. By committing to resolve conflicts with compassion and clarity, you foster a resilient bond that can withstand the challenges that come, fortified by the knowledge and skills you gain with each resolved disagreement.

4.4 Building Trust Through Consistency and Reliability

Trust is the bedrock upon which secure and enduring relationships are built. Feeling safe and secure with another person allows us to open up, share our innermost thoughts, and connect. But trust isn't just about big gestures or promises; it's built through consistent, reliable behaviors in day-to-day interactions. When trust is present, relationships flourish under its protective and nurturing influence. Even the most minor crack can feel like a chasm when absent.

Building trust starts with consistency. Being consistent means that your words match your actions. If you say you will call at a certain time, you do. You show up if you promise to be there when your friend or partner needs you. This reliability in small matters lays a foundation of trust, reassuring the other person that they can rely on you in more significant issues. It's like placing stones in a foundation, one at a time, each one strengthening the structure. Over time, this consistency in your actions reassures your partner that you are dependable, essential for creating a secure emotional environment.

Being emotionally available is another crucial aspect of building trust. It means being present with your partner, ready to listen and respond to their needs without judgment. When you are emotionally available, you engage with genuine interest and empathy, providing a safe space for your partner to express their feelings and vulnerabilities. This openness fosters deeper intimacy, as both partners feel seen and understood, further cementing their trust. Emotional availability isn't about having all the answers; it's about being there, thoroughly and attentively, through the joys and the challenges.

Rebuilding trust where it has been damaged is a more delicate process. Perhaps a misunderstanding led to disappointment or a mistake that hurt the other person deeply. Rebuilding trust in these situations requires patience, humility, and a commitment to healing whatever wounds were inflicted. Start by acknowledging the hurt your actions may have caused. This acknowledgment is crucial because it shows you take their feelings seriously and understand the gravity of the situation. Following this, it's important to take responsibility without making excuses. This demonstrates your willingness to own your part in what happened.

Next, engage in open dialogue about what changes can be made to avoid similar issues in the future. This conversation should be a two-way street, allowing both parties to express their needs and concerns. As you implement these changes, remember that rebuilding trust is a gradual process. Each step taken should be viewed as a brick in rebuilding your relationship's foundation. Be patient with yourself and your partner, and celebrate small victories. Over time, these efforts can restore lost trust, leading to a stronger and more resilient relationship.

Lastly, the development of self-trust is an essential component of this process. Self-trust means having confidence in your own decisions and feelings. It requires you to listen to and honor your inner voice, especially when it tells you what you need in a relationship or what boundaries need to be set. Developing self-trust can be a transformative experience, as it empowers you to interact with others from a place of strength and assurance. To enhance your self-trust, engage regularly in self-reflection. Consider how your actions align with your values and whether your decisions reflect what you truly believe and desire. Self-reflection helps make more authentic decisions and reinforces your trust in your ability to care for and protect your emotional well-being.

Practices like journaling or mindfulness can facilitate this self-reflection, providing insights into your thought patterns and emotional reactions. These practices help you become more attuned to your intuitive feelings about people and situations, guiding you towards choices that respect and enhance your well-being. As you develop stronger self-trust, it naturally extends to your relationships, enabling you to trust others more freely and deeply. This trust, built on self-assurance and mutual respect, creates a dynamic where both partners feel safe and valued, ready to grow together.

4.5 The Role of Independence in Fostering Secure Relationships

In the delicate dance of intimacy, where each step towards closer connection can sometimes feel like a potential loss of self, understanding the balance between autonomy and deep emotional connections is crucial. Maintaining your individuality brings strength and diversity to your relationships, enriching them rather than diluting your personal essence Independence in a relationship does not signify emotional distance but rather a harmonious blend where both partners support each other's growth and pursuits. This balance is essential, as it ensures that the relationship enhances each person's life, making it more fulfilling rather than restrictive.

The journey towards fostering this balance begins with nurturing your independence, foundational to your sense of self. Engaging in activities that resonate with your interests and values is vital. Whether pursuing a hobby, advancing your career, or cultivating spiritual practices, these activities should be nurtured without the fear of losing connection with your partner. By dedicating time to your passions and interests, you enrich your life and bring new energies and insights back into your relationship, keeping it dynamic and engaging. Moreover, cultivating financial independence and self-reliance is equally essential. Being financially secure and capable of managing your affairs independently instills a profound sense of self-efficacy and confidence, naturally alleviating pressures and dependencies in your relationships and fostering a healthier dynamic.

Developing a solid sense of self and independence is crucial in mitigating fears often accompanying attachment, such as the fear of abandonment or the anxiety of being too needy. When you are comfortable with yourself and are fulfilled in your pursuits, the fear of abandonment diminishes. You know that you can be content with your company and that your happiness does not depend solely on another person. Similarly, by being self-reliant, you avoid placing excessive emotional demands on your partner, which can often lead to feeling overwhelmed or trapped in the relationship. This self-sufficiency fosters a healthier, more balanced relationship dynamic where both partners feel equally invested and independent yet profoundly connected.

Supporting your partner's independence is equally crucial. It involves respecting their need for personal space and time for their activities and interests. Encourage your partner to pursue what brings them joy and fulfillment outside the relationship. This support shows your love and respect for their individuality and strengthens the relationship by promoting mutual respect and admiration. It's important to communicate openly about each other's needs for independence and to make adjustments as necessary to ensure that both partners feel supported yet free to grow. This might involve setting aside time where each partner can pursue personal interests or agreeing on certain boundaries that help maintain a healthy balance of togetherness and separateness.

In essence, fostering independence within a relationship is about creating a supportive environment where both partners can grow individually and together. It's about celebrating each other's successes and supporting their endeavors without feeling threatened or neglected. This balance of autonomy and connection enriches the relationship, making it more resilient and satisfying. As you and your partner support each other's independence, you build a deeper trust and respect that forms the cornerstone of a lasting, secure relationship. This mutual support enhances the quality of your relationship and contributes to a fulfilling life where both partners can thrive individually and as a couple.

4.6 Transitioning from Anxious to Secure: Real Stories of Change

The path from anxious to secure attachment often unfolds uniquely for everyone, yet it is paved with universal milestones of self-discovery, challenges, and profound personal growth. Through the lens of real-life experiences, we can glean powerful insights that inspire and guide us in our own processes of emotional transformation. Let's explore the journeys of three individuals who have successfully navigated the shift from deep-seated anxiety in their relationships to a place of greater security and confidence.

First, consider the story of Maya, who spent most of her twenties in a succession of turbulent relationships, driven by her fears of abandonment and rejection. Her turning point came after a particularly painful breakup, which propelled her into therapy. There, she uncovered the roots of her anxious attachment—early childhood experiences of inconsistent parenting. The critical lesson from Maya's journey was the importance of self-awareness. Through therapy, she learned to recognize and understand her triggers, which were essential first steps toward healing. She began practicing mindfulness to stay present during moments of insecurity instead of spiraling into fear. Over time, Maya's new awareness and coping strategies fostered a greater sense of security within herself, which gradually mirrored her relationships.

Then, there's Liam, whose story highlights the power of persistence. Liam's anxious attachment manifested in a constant need for reassurance from his partners, which often overwhelmed his relationships. His journey began with acknowledging his insecurities and their detrimental impact on his relationships. The process could have been quicker and more accessible, involving several starts and stops. However, Liam's commitment to change remained strong. He engaged in regular counseling, joined support groups, and dedicated himself to personal development books and exercises. Through persistent effort, Liam learned to cultivate his self-worth independently from his relationships, significantly alleviating his need for external validation.

Another profound narrative is that of Elena, who discovered the importance of a support system in her journey towards secure attachment. After enduring a volatile relationship that exacerbated her anxious tendencies, Elena felt isolated and misunderstood. The breakthrough came when she reached out to a friend who had faced similar challenges. This friend introduced her to a community of individuals who shared their experiences and coping strategies. The support and understanding she received were instrumental in her healing process. Elena learned she wasn't alone in her fears and that sharing her experiences could be incredibly validating and empowering. This communal support was crucial for Elena as it provided not only practical strategies for managing her anxiety but also emotional reassurance that she was on the right path.

These stories underscore common themes crucial for transitioning from anxious to secure attachment. Self-awareness helps identify personal triggers and understand how past experiences influence current behaviors. Persistence is vital in continuing the effort toward change, even when progress seems slow or invisible. Support systems provide the necessary encouragement and validation to persevere through the challenges. Each story is a testament to the power of resilience and the possibility of transformation.

This chapter's narratives illuminate the profound empowerment of moving towards secure attachment. Each individual's success reinforces that change is possible, not just in the abstract, but in life's tangible, sometimes messy realities. They remind us that while the road to security is often fraught with challenges, it is also lined with opportunities for growth, self-discovery, and deeper connections.

As we close this chapter, remember that your journey toward secure attachment, while uniquely yours, shares the universal themes of self-awareness, persistence, and the crucial role of support systems. These stories are mirrors reflecting not only your potential struggles but also your potential triumphs. As we transition into the next chapter, keep these narratives in mind—they are not just stories but roadmaps that can guide you towards a more secure, fulfilled relational life.

Make a Difference with Your Review

Unlock the Power of Generosity

"True happiness comes from helping others." - Unknown

Did you know that people who help others are often happier and more successful? That's why I'm reaching out to you today.

I have a question for you...

Would you help someone you've never met, even if you never got credit?

Who is this person? They are like you, or maybe like you used to be. They want to understand their feelings better, build stronger relationships, and feel more secure. But they need a little guidance to get there.

Our mission is to make Anxious Attachment Recovery accessible to everyone. Everything I do is to help more people find peace and confidence in their relationships. But I can't do it alone. I need your help to reach more people.

This is where you come in. Many people decide to read a book based on its reviews. So here's my request for a person struggling with relationships who you've never met:

Please help that person by leaving a review for this book.

Your review won't cost you anything and will take less than 60 seconds to write, but it could change someone's life forever.

Simply scan the QR code below to leave your review:

Thank you from the bottom of my heart. Now, let's get back to the book.

- Take Care, Anne Moigis

Chapter 5

Advanced Self-Reflection and Growth

I magine walking through a dense forest where the path is unclear, and every step forward requires you to push the branches aside gently. Each branch represents a reaction or a habit that has shaped how you interact in your relationships, especially those tinted by the hues of anxious attachment. This chapter is about pausing in that walk, examining each branch closely, and choosing whether to let it snap back into place or gently reshape its path, creating a new way forward that reflects your growth and newfound understanding.

5.1 Recognizing Triggers and Deconstructing Reactions

Identifying Emotional Triggers

Navigating through the forest of our emotions, we often stumble upon hidden triggers—those deeply ingrained reactions that seem to launch us into a state of anxiety without a moment's notice. Identifying these triggers is like mapping the hidden roots that trip us up. Start by reflecting on recent moments when you felt overwhelmed or anxious in a relationship. What specific event or interaction preceded that feeling? Perhaps it was a delayed response from a friend, a partner's offhand comment, or a particular date that holds historical significance in your emotional calendar.

Creating a 'trigger journal' can be an effective strategy here. Whenever you feel that rush of anxiety, jot down the context, the people involved, and what was said or done. Over time, patterns will emerge, revealing the specific conditions that ignite your anxious attachments. This journal becomes your guide, illuminating the often subconscious pathways that lead to distress. It empowers you to anticipate and prepare for these reactions rather than being blindsided by them.

Understanding the Why

With your triggers identified, the next step is to explore the 'why' behind each. This exploration involves delving into the beliefs and fears that fuel your reactions. For instance, if you discover that you're triggered by your partner spending time with others, it might reflect a more profound fear of being replaced or not valued. These fears often stem from past experiences where you felt abandoned or sidelined.

Understanding these underlying fears requires a compassionate inward dive, where you gently question the origin of these beliefs without self-judgment. Ask yourself, "What experiences are informing this reaction?" and "What might my emotional self be trying to protect me from?" This understanding can shift your perspective from seeing these reactions as overreactions to recognizing them as protective measures your mind has put in place. They are not flaws but signs of wounds that need care and reassurance.

Mindful Observation

Once you understand what triggers you and why, it is vital to practice observing your reactions without immediately acting on them. This is where mindfulness, a practice rooted in maintaining a moment-by-moment awareness of our thoughts, feelings, bodily sensations, and surrounding environment, comes into play. When you feel triggered, try to pause and observe your thoughts and feelings as if you were an external bystander. This detachment allows you to see your reactions without being overwhelmed by them.

A practical method to enhance this mindful observation is the 'STOP' technique:

- S: Stop what you are doing.

- T: Take a few deep breaths.

- O: Observe your thoughts, feelings, and bodily sensations.

- P: Proceed with more awareness and compassion.

Practicing this technique can help you gain important moments to choose how you wish to respond rather than being swept away by the initial impulse.

Transforming Reactions

The final step in this journey of self-reflection is transforming these automatic reactions into thoughtful responses. This transformation doesn't happen overnight but through consistent practice and commitment to growth. Begin by identifying alternative responses that align more closely with your desired way of being in relationships. For example, suppose your instinct is to send a barrage of messages when you feel ignored. In that case, you might choose instead to engage in an activity that you enjoy, giving your partner space while addressing your anxiety.

Visualization can be a powerful too here. Envision yourself successfully handling a situation that would typically trigger an anxious response. See yourself responding in a way that reflects your growth—calm, collected, and compassionate. Rehearse this new response in your mind until it begins to feel more natural. The more you practice, the more you rewire your brain's habitual reactions, making it easier to adopt these healthier responses in real situations.

Transforming your reactions is not about suppressing your true feelings but responding to them in ways that honor your needs and relationships. It's about choosing to respond rather than react, bringing your most wise self to the moments when it's most needed.

5.2 The Art of Self-Forgiveness in the Healing Process

Self-forgiveness is a vital aspect of personal growth and healing, especially when navigating the complexities of relationships influenced by anxious attachment. Imagine carrying a backpack filled with stones, each representing a past mistake or a harsh self-judgment you've directed at yourself. Over time, this load can become unbearable, hindering your movement forward and affecting your relationships. Self-forgiveness involves unpacking these stones, examining them, and choosing to set them aside, not because they weren't heavy or painful, but because you recognize that carrying them won't change the past nor define your future.

The importance of self-forgiveness in the healing process cannot be overstated. It allows you to acknowledge your imperfections and accept that mistakes, no matter their nature, are part of the human experience, not indicators of your worth or capabilities. For those grappling with anxious attachment, where fears of rejection and abandonment can drive behavior that you might later regret, self-forgiveness becomes essential. It helps to soften the often harsh internal dialogue that can accompany these regrets, replacing self-criticism with a more nurturing and supportive voice. When you forgive yourself, you acknowledge that while you may have acted out of fear, these actions do not solely define you, and you deserve compassion and understanding from yourself as much as from others.

Overcoming self-judgment is a crucial step in the process of self-forgiveness. It begins by recognizing the critical inner voice that amplifies your perceived flaws or mistakes. This voice might often replay your less-than-ideal reactions or decisions, especially those that affect your relationships, convincing you that you are doomed to repeat these patterns. Challenging this voice involves consciously noticing when it arises and actively countering its messages with evidence of your positive qualities and achievements. Instead of letting it dominate your self-perception, you can see it as an old defense mechanism that no longer serves you. Replacing this critical voice with one that speaks from a place of understanding and kindness can transform your relationship with yourself and, by extension, with others.

Forgiveness exercises can be powerful tools in facilitating the process of self-forgiveness. One effective practice is letter writing, where you write a letter to yourself discussing a specific incident or behavior you regret. In this letter, express everything you feel without holding back. Then, shift the narrative to one of forgiveness and understanding. Highlight your human nature, growth capacity, and worthiness of love and forgiveness. This exercise allows emotional release and helps solidify a more compassionate self-view. Another helpful practice is guided meditation focused on forgiveness. These meditations can lead you through visualizations of releasing past burdens and can instill a more profound sense of peace and forgiveness toward yourself.

The ongoing nature of self-forgiveness is something that requires recognition and commitment. Unlike a one-time event, self-forgiveness is a practice that needs to be revisited often, especially as new layers of understanding or old memories surface. Regularly dedicating time to reflect on your self-talk and to engage in forgiveness practices can reinforce a state of self-compassion. Setting aside specific times in your routine for this purpose is helpful, treating them as essential appointments with yourself. Over time, these moments of self-forgiveness will lighten your emotional load and enhance your capacity to engage in healthier, more secure relationships. Through continuous practice, self-forgiveness becomes less of an occasional remedy and a default mode of engaging with yourself—a fundamental part of a life lived with compassion and grace.

5.3 Reclaiming Your Narrative: Empowerment Through Storytelling

The stories we weave about ourselves and our experiences are not just idle tales; they shape the fabric of our identities and influence how we interact with the world and form relationships. Whether empowering or limiting, each narrative we hold dear acts as a lens through which we perceive our reality. When these narratives center around themes of anxiety, loss, or inadequacy—common in those with anxious attachment styles—they can distort our perceptions and interactions, reinforcing feelings of insecurity and fear. However, by actively reclaiming and reshaping these narratives, you can redefine your identity and enhance your relationship dynamics.

Consider the narratives you currently tell about past relationships or your worthiness of love and belonging. There may be stories you recall that paint you as always the one left behind or as someone not quite good enough. These stories, often born from painful experiences, might have once been a protective shield, helping you make sense of hurtful events. Yet, when held too tightly, they can hinder your growth and impede the development of secure attachments. To transform these narratives, identify the disempowering stories you've been telling yourself. Reflect on their origins and the impact they've had on your life. This reflection isn't about assigning blame but understanding the context in which these narratives were formed.

The next step involves reframing these stories to highlight your resilience and growth rather than your pain and setbacks. This reframing is not about denying past hurt but changing the story's focus to emphasize your strengths and triumphs. For instance, instead of a narrative that focuses on your struggles with abandonment, you might reframe it to highlight how these experiences have cultivated in you a deep capacity for empathy and understanding. By shifting the narrative in this way, you alter how you view your past and how you approach current and future relationships.

Storytelling as a tool for empowerment involves rethinking your personal narratives and actively using your stories to inspire and connect with others. Writing your experiences down, whether in a private journal or a blog, transforms abstract feelings and thoughts into concrete expressions of your journey. This act of creation can be incredibly validating and healing. It allows you to take ownership of your experiences and to see them as integral parts of your life's tapestry, each with valuable lessons and insights.

Sharing your story with others can further enhance this healing process. Whether in support groups, through social media, or in more intimate settings like family gatherings or with friends, sharing your journey can be profoundly liberating. It not only helps dissipate any shame or isolation associated with your experiences but also opens up avenues for connection with others navigating similar paths. When you share your story, you offer it as a bridge, inviting others to meet you in a place of vulnerability and mutual understanding. In these shared spaces, stories weave a collective fabric of human experience, rich with the threads of challenge, resilience, and hope.

In embracing the power of narrative, you empower yourself to author a new chapter in your life, where past pains are transformed into sources of strength and wisdom. This narrative reclamation is not a one-time edit but an ongoing process of revisiting and revising your life story as you continue to grow and evolve. Each iteration reflects a deeper understanding of who you are and how you relate to the world, paving the way for relationships that are rooted in authenticity and secured by mutual respect and understanding. Through this dynamic and conscious engagement with your narrative, you reclaim your story and your life, opening up new possibilities for love, connection, and fulfillment.

5.4 Setting Healthy Personal and Emotional Boundaries

The art of setting boundaries is akin to planting a garden where each boundary is like a small fence around your most cherished plants—it protects and nurtures, allowing them to thrive. Boundaries serve a similar purpose in the landscape of personal well-being and relationships. They safeguard your emotional space, filter out undue stress or demands, and foster a healthy, respectful environment where secure attachments can flourish. Understanding and setting these boundaries are not just acts of self-care; they are declarations of your self-worth and essential tools for nurturing healthy relationships.

Boundaries come in various forms, and their necessity spans across different aspects of your life, including physical spaces, emotional energies, and time commitments. To identify where boundaries might be needed or require strengthening, start by reflecting on aspects of your life where you feel discomfort, resentment, or exhaustion. These feelings often signal that your limits are pushed, ignored, or unacknowledged. For instance, if you consistently find yourself overwhelmed by social engagements, it might indicate a need for more precise boundaries around your time and social commitments. Similarly, if certain interactions consistently leave you emotionally drained, it might be time to set boundaries around your emotional availability or the conversations you want to engage in.

Once you've identified these areas, the next step is clearly defining what these boundaries need to look like. This process involves honest self-reflection about what you value, what you can handle comfortably, and what is non-negotiable for your mental health and happiness. For example, if you value quiet time in the evenings to recharge, setting a boundary might involve no phone calls or visitors after a particular hour. Or, if discussing work issues at home disrupts your peace, you might need to establish a boundary that work-related conversations are off-limits during family time.

Communicating your boundaries clearly and assertively is crucial. It involves expressing your needs respectfully and directly, without apology. When communicating your boundaries, use "I" statements that reflect your needs and feelings without blaming or criticizing others. For example, say, "I need some quiet evening time to unwind. I would appreciate it if we could schedule serious discussions earlier." This approach shows that you are taking responsibility for your needs and also respect the listener by giving them clear information on how they can respect your boundaries.

Respecting others' boundaries is equally essential and reflects the mutual respect required for healthy relationship dynamics. Pay attention to verbal and non-verbal cues that indicate others' boundaries. If someone seems uncomfortable or hesitant about a particular topic or interaction, stepping back and respecting their limits is essential. Actively asking about and acknowledging others' boundaries can also foster an environment of mutual respect and care. For example, asking a friend, "Are you comfortable discussing this topic right now, or would you prefer to talk about something else?" gives them the autonomy to set boundaries, reinforcing a healthy dynamic in their relationship.

In practicing these steps, you protect your emotional well-being and lay the groundwork for relationships based on mutual respect and understanding. Setting and respecting boundaries might initially feel challenging, especially if you're used to putting others' needs before yours. However, with time and practice, it becomes an integral part of how you interact with the world, ensuring that your relationships are supportive and empowering. As you continue to navigate through your interactions with more precise boundaries, you likely find that your relationships are healthier and have more energy and respect for yourself and others, creating a cycle of positive interactions and deepening connections.

5.5 Cultivating Emotional Intelligence for Better Relationships

Emotional Intelligence (EI), a term first popularized by psychologist Daniel Goleman, involves being aware of, controlling, and expressing one's emotions and handling interpersonal relationships judiciously and empathetically. This multifaceted concept encompasses several core skills: self-awareness, self-regulation, empathy, and social skills. Each of these components plays a crucial role in developing and maintaining healthy, secure relationships.

Defining Emotional Intelligence (EI)

Self-awareness is recognizing and understanding your emotions and how they affect your thoughts and behavior. This awareness allows you to understand your emotional triggers and recognize when your emotions might cloud your judgment. Self-regulation, closely tied to self-awareness, involves managing your emotions healthily, adapting to changing circumstances, and following through on commitments. Meanwhile, empathy refers to the ability to understand the feelings of others, an essential skill for building solid and empathetic connections with partners, friends, and colleagues. Lastly, social skills involve communicating, influencing others, managing conflict, and working well in a team, which are crucial for successful interpersonal interactions.

EI and Attachment

The link between emotional intelligence and the development of secure attachment styles is profound. High EI can mitigate the intensity of anxieties typically associated with insecure attachment styles by enhancing your understanding of your emotional landscape and improving how you relate to others. For instance, self-awareness allows you to recognize when feelings of insecurity might lead to clinginess or withdrawal in relationships. With this awareness, you can use self-regulation techniques to calm your anxieties and respond in a way that fosters connection rather than conflict. Empathy deepens this connection by enabling you to perceive and respond to your partner's emotional state, promoting a mutual understanding foundational to secure attachment. Additionally, practical social skills allow you to clearly communicate your needs and feelings, negotiate boundaries, and seek support, strengthening relational bonds.

Building EI Skills

Enhancing your emotional intelligence involves intentional practice across its different components. To boost your self-awareness, engage in regular self-reflection. This could include taking time daily to reflect on your emotional responses to other interactions and what these might say about your underlying needs or fears. Journaling can be a particularly effective tool, allowing you to track patterns over time and gain deeper insights into your emotional triggers.

Improving self-regulation might involve developing and practicing relaxation techniques such as deep breathing, meditation, or progressive muscle relaxation. These methods can help calm emotional intensity, allowing you to respond more thoughtfully in stressful situations. To enhance your empathy, try to consciously practice putting yourself in others' shoes in everyday situations. This could be as simple as imagining the feelings of a coworker who seems stressed or considering the perspective of a friend who has shared a problem with you.

To develop your social skills, focus on active listening and clear communication. Active listening involves fully concentrating on what is being said rather than passively hearing the speaker's message. It includes listening with all senses and giving full attention to the speaker. Clear communication means expressing your thoughts and feelings openly and honestly, without aggression or passivity. This might involve practicing expressing your needs and feelings effectively or assertively expressing disagreement without undermining the other person's perspective.

Applying EI in Relationships

The application of enhanced emotional intelligence in relationships can transform interactions profoundly. For instance, increased self-awareness and regulation can prevent misunderstandings that arise from misinterpreted emotions or poorly managed stress. In a practical sense, this might mean recognizing that your irritability at the end of a stressful workday is more about your state of mind than about your partner's actions. By acknowledging this, you can engage in a stress-reducing activity before addressing any relationship issues, thus preventing unnecessary conflict.

Empathy allows you to be more attuned to your partner's emotional needs and to respond in ways that validate and support them, deepening your emotional connection. For example, suppose your partner is upset about a difficult work situation instead of immediately offering solutions. In that case, you might first acknowledge their feelings and express understanding of their frustration, making them feel heard and cared for.

Lastly, refined social skills can improve one's ability to resolve conflicts effectively, negotiate needs, and maintain fulfilling interpersonal relationships. This might involve using conflict resolution strategies that focus on finding solutions that meet both partners' needs, fostering teamwork, and sharing goals within the relationship.

You create a robust framework for developing and maintaining secure, fulfilling relationships by continually practicing and applying these EI skills. This framework supports your personal growth and enriches your connections with others, creating a network of relationships built on mutual understanding, respect, and emotional support.

5.6 From Insight to Action: Making Meaningful Changes

Transforming the insights gained from deep self-reflection into tangible, every-day actions is a pivotal step in your path toward personal growth and healthier relationships. It's one thing to understand your emotional patterns and another to actively shift them in ways that lead to more fulfilling interactions and a greater sense of well-being. This transformative process involves a deliberate, thoughtful approach to integrating new behaviors and thought patterns into your life, ensuring that your changes are effective and sustainable.

Translating Insights into Behaviors

The bridge between insight and action is built on applying your new under-standing in real-life situations. For instance, if you've recognized that you tend to react defensively when feeling insecure, the next step is implementing a different behavior when this feeling arises. Instead of immediately responding, you might pause, acknowledge your feelings internally, and choose a response that aligns with your desire for open communication and connection. This could mean expressing your feelings calmly to your partner or asking for a moment to collect your thoughts.

Implementing these changes requires mindfulness and patience, as old habits can persist. One effective technique to facilitate this shift is using reminders or cues. Set a reminder on your phone that pops up daily with a prompt to practice a new response, or keep a note on your fridge that reminds you of your commitment to change. These small cues can help keep your new goals top-of-mind, gently nudging you towards your desired behavior patterns.

Setting Achievable Goals

Goal setting is a powerful tool in your journey of personal transformation, providing clear targets to aim for and a sense of direction. When setting goals related to your attachment and personal development, it's crucial to ensure they are realistic and achievable. Start by breaking larger goals into smaller, manageable steps. For example, if your goal is to become more secure in your relationships, a smaller, achievable goal might be to express your needs openly in one daily interaction.

Each small goal should be specific and measurable, making it clear what you're aiming for and allowing you to track your progress. Additionally, ensure your goals are time-bound, giving yourself a realistic deadline. This structure helps maintain your motivation, providing regular checkpoints to celebrate your progress and reassess your approach if needed.

Action Plans

Creating a detailed action plan is your roadmap to making meaningful changes. This plan outlines what you aim to achieve and how you will go about it, including the strategies you will use and the resources you might need. Start by writing down your overall goal, then list the steps you believe will get you there. Each step should include specific actions, such as practicing a new communication skill or attending a therapy session.

Your action plan should also consider potential obstacles and how you might overcome them. For example, if your goal is to react less defensively to criticism, a possible obstacle might be your automatic emotional response. A strategy to overcome this could be to practice deep breathing techniques to manage your initial emotional reaction, allowing you to respond more thoughtfully.

Celebrating Small Wins

As you progress towards your goals, acknowledge and celebrate each achievement, no matter how small. These celebrations are essential for building momentum and maintaining motivation. Each small win is a building block in your more significant growth journey, reinforcing that your efforts are paying off and bringing you closer to your desired outcome.

Celebrating can be as simple as reflecting on what you've achieved and sharing this with a friend or loved one to affirm your progress. You might also treat yourself to something you enjoy, like a favorite meal or a relaxing evening, as a reward for your hard work. These moments of celebration make the process enjoyable and sustainable, infusing your journey with positive reinforcement.

In integrating these strategies, you transform the insights gained from your reflections into active steps toward a more secure and fulfilling life. This chapter serves as a guide to help you navigate this process, providing practical tools and encouragement to support you in turning your newfound understanding into concrete changes. As you move forward, each small step and achieved goal weaves together to form a more decadent, more resilient fabric of your life, ultimately leading to deeper connections and a more profound sense of self.

Moving Forward

As this chapter concludes, reflect on the insights and strategies discussed here and consider how they can be applied to foster growth and positive change in your daily life. Remember, the journey of personal development is ongoing, and each step you take builds upon the last, leading to greater understanding and fulfillment. Applying these principles will pave the way for more secure attachments and a richer, more connected life. Looking ahead, the next chapter will explore strategies for maintaining and nurturing these positive changes, ensuring that the growth you achieve is sustained and continues to enrich your life.

Chapter 6

Nurturing Emotional Resilience

I magine standing at the edge of a vast, serene lake, the surface a perfect mirror reflecting the sky above. The calmness of the water belies the depth and complexity beneath, much like the surface of our emotional resilience. Just as the lake's calm waters can absorb disturbances with gentle ripples before returning to tranquility, a resilient mindset allows us to navigate the ebbs and flows of emotional challenges with grace and strength. Emotional resilience isn't about avoiding distress or sidestepping adversity; instead, it's about embracing life's challenges with perseverance and transformation, enabling us to emerge stronger and more grounded.

6.1 The Foundations of Emotional Resilience

Understanding Resilience

Emotional resilience can be envisioned as the psychological equivalent of an immune system. Just as our biological defenses protect against illness, resilience protects us against the psychological strains of life's stresses. It's about more than just bouncing back; it involves growth and personal betterment from experiences that might otherwise overwhelm us. For those grappling with anxious attachment, resilience offers a pathway to not only recover but also thrive, transforming reactive patterns into proactive steps toward emotional well-being.

Core Components

At the heart of resilience lie three critical attributes: flexibility, perseverance, and optimism. Flexibility involves adapting to changing situations and adjusting one's approach to tackling problems. It allows you to bend without breaking when pressures mount. Perseverance, the second attribute, is about maintaining a steady path forward despite setbacks and frustrations. It's the quiet determination that fuels continued effort after disappointment. Optimism, the third component, is not about naive cheerfulness but rather the ability to maintain hope and find meaningful lessons amid difficulty.

Building a Resilient Mindset

Developing a resilient mindset is akin to strengthening a muscle—it grows through consistent practice and dedication. One powerful method is cognitive reframing, which involves changing your perspective on negative experiences, viewing them as opportunities for learning and growth rather than insurmountable obstacles. For instance, instead of viewing a relationship setback as a failure, see it as a chance to deepen your understanding of your needs and attachment patterns. Acceptance also plays a crucial role here; it's about recognizing the reality of a situation without resistance or denial. Acceptance allows you to conserve emotional energy and focus on what you can change rather than lamenting what you cannot.

Resilience and Attachment

The development of emotional resilience significantly bolsters the journey towards secure attachment. Resilient individuals are better equipped to handle the uncertainties and anxieties of building and maintaining relationships. They can navigate close relationships' natural highs and lows without retreating into old anxious attachment patterns. Moreover, resilience fosters a sense of inner security, reducing dependency on others for emotional validation and support. This independence enhances personal growth and contributes to healthier, more balanced relationships.

Cultivating resilience is particularly empowering for individuals with anxious attachment styles. It provides a set of emotional tools that can transform their approach to relationships and life's challenges. By nurturing resilience, you learn to manage your attachment anxieties more effectively and enhance your overall quality of life, making you better equipped to pursue fulfilling relationships and personal goals. Through resilience, the rough waters of emotional challenges are navigated with greater ease and the calm, like that of the serene lake, becomes more profound and sustaining.

6.2 Creating a Personal Resilience Plan

In the delicate art of cultivating personal resilience, understanding your unique emotional landscape is the first step. Each of us carries a distinct set of experiences, strengths, and areas that may need nurturing. Begin by assessing where you currently stand in terms of resilience. Reflect on recent situations that challenged your emotional balance: how did you respond? Did you feel overwhelmed, or could you navigate these challenges with a measure of calm and perspective? This isn't about judging yourself harshly but observing with kindness and curiosity. Identify patterns in your reactions that might signal areas for growth—perhaps you notice a tendency to withdraw in conflict situations or difficulty bouncing back from disappointment.

With this self-awareness, you're ready to design your personal resilience plan. This plan is not a rigid set of rules but a living document that evolves with you. Start by setting clear, achievable goals that address your specific resilience needs. For instance, if maintaining emotional balance during stress is challenging, a goal might be practicing mindfulness for ten minutes each day. Incorporate both daily practices and long-term strategies: daily practices could include journaling or affirmations, while long-term strategies might involve regular therapy sessions or attending a support group. Ensure that your goals are specific enough to be actionable and measurable, which will help track your progress and make adjustments as needed.

Support systems play a critical role in building and sustaining resilience. They provide emotional support, perspective, and feedback that can be crucial in challenging times. Lean into your relationships—reach out to friends, family, or colleagues who understand and support your journey. If your current circle is limited, consider expanding by joining clubs, classes, or online communities to connect with others with similar goals and interests. Remember, the strength of your support system lies not just in the number of people but in the quality of connections and the mutual support they offer.

Regularly reviewing and adapting your resilience plan is essential. As you grow and your circumstances change, your needs and your plan will evolve. Set a regular interval for review—monthly or quarterly might work—and ask yourself what's working and what isn't during each review. Are there new challenges that need to be addressed? Have specific strategies become less effective? This is also a time to celebrate your progress and recalibrate your goals. Adjusting your plan isn't a sign of setback but a natural part of your growth process, reflecting your more profound understanding of yourself and your resilience needs.

By actively engaging in this process, you empower yourself to manage life's challenges with a more robust, more resilient outlook. This proactive approach enhances your ability to cope with stress and adversity. It enriches your overall life experience, allowing you to engage with the world from a place of strength and confidence. Your personal resilience plan becomes your roadmap, guiding you through the complexities of life with a renewed sense of purpose and stability.

6.3 Strategies for Coping with Relationship Anxiety

In the dance of intimacy and connection, anxiety often steps in uninvited, casting shadows of doubt and fear over our relationships. It can sneak into moments of Vulnerability, whisper insecurities during times of silence, and amplify misinterpretations in communication. Understanding the sources of this anxiety is the first step towards managing it effectively. These anxieties often stem from past experiences, perhaps from early relationships where emotional needs were unmet or loss and disappointment left deep imprints. They may also arise from personal fears of inadequacy or the pressure of societal expectations that dictate how relationships 'should' work. Recognizing these patterns lets you see that your anxieties are not reflections of your current relationship's reality but echoes of past pains and ingrained fears.

A variety of coping mechanisms can be employed to navigate these turbulent waters. One effective strategy is to develop what I like to call an 'emotional first aid kit.' This kit involves a collection of personal strategies that can help soothe your anxiety when it flares. Techniques might include deep breathing exercises, which help calm the nervous system and reduce the immediate physical symptoms of anxiety. Another tool could be visualization, where you imagine a place that makes you feel safe and peaceful, helping to restore your mental focus and emotional balance. Creating a list of affirmations that reinforce your self-worth and the positive aspects of your relationship can also be helpful. These affirmations serve as reminders of the truth about your relationships and your value in them, helping to counteract the negative, intrusive thoughts that fuel anxiety.

When rooted in honesty and clarity, communication can significantly alleviate relationship anxiety. It involves expressing your feelings openly and honestly without fear of judgment. When you share your fears and vulnerabilities with your partner, it not only lifts the burden of carrying them alone but also allows your partner to understand your needs and anxieties better. Effective communication involves active listening and fully engaging with your partner's words without planning your response or making assumptions. This practice helps to clear misunderstandings and build a deeper connection, as both partners feel genuinely heard and understood. Setting regular times to check in with each other about the relationship can create a safe space for these important conversations, ensuring that minor issues don't build into larger anxieties.

Self-care is crucial in managing relationship anxiety. It's about nurturing yourself for your well-being and maintaining your emotional health, which directly impacts your relationship. Self-care practices include regular physical activity, which helps release endorphins and improves mood, or engaging in hobbies that bring you joy and fulfillment outside your relationship. Ensuring that you have time alone can also be incredibly beneficial, allowing you space to reconnect with yourself and maintain your identity. This helps prevent the relationship from becoming your sole source of emotional fulfillment, which can intensify anxiety. Regular mindfulness or meditation practices can also be invaluable. They teach you to stay present in the moment rather than getting lost in worries about the future or regrets about the past, reducing stress and fostering a calm mind.

Employing these strategies not only helps manage anxiety but also strengthens your relationship. It allows you to interact from a place of strength and clarity, free from the constraints of unchecked anxieties. By taking proactive steps to understand and cope with your relationship anxiety, you create a healthier, more nurturing environment for you and your partner. This approach doesn't just mitigate the symptoms of anxiety but addresses its roots, paving the way for a deeper, more satisfying connection. As you continue to apply these strategies, they become more intuitive, transforming how you cope with anxiety and how you experience love and connection in your relationship.

6.4 Embracing Vulnerability as a Strength

Vulnerability often carries a veil of misconception, portrayed as a sign of weakness or a gateway to emotional hurt. Yet, what if we peel back this veil and see Vulnerability for what it can be—a profound strength and a cornerstone for deep, meaningful connections? In a world that frequently urges us to armor up against any potential emotional risk, choosing Vulnerability is an act of courage. It involves peeling off the layers of self-protection we've built around our hearts and daring to let others see us in our authentic state. This openness is not about reckless emotional exposure but about selectively sharing our innermost thoughts, feelings, and desires with those we trust and care about, fostering a closer, more genuine connection.

The strength of vulnerability lies in its ability to deepen connections. When you share your fears, hopes, or dreams with someone, you are not just sharing words but inviting them into a more intimate emotional space. This act can transform relationships, creating a bond built on trust and mutual understanding, the kind that can weather the storms of life. When both people in a relationship can express their vulnerabilities, it creates a dynamic of mutual support and validation. Each person feels seen and valued for their strengths, uncertainties, and imperfections, which are universal aspects of the human experience.

Practicing vulnerability, however, requires thoughtful navigation. It involves knowing when and with whom to open up, which is crucial in maintaining emotional safety. Setting boundaries around vulnerability means understanding your comfort levels and communicating them clearly to others. For instance, specific topics are off-limits for discussion in larger groups but are open for sharing in one-on-one settings or with close friends. It's also about pacing—divulging personal information gradually as trust is built rather than all at once. By setting these boundaries, you create a safe space for vulnerability, where you can express your true self without fear of judgment or misunderstanding.

For many, the fear of vulnerability stems from past experiences where openness led to hurt or rejection. Overcoming this fear begins with recognizing that past experiences, while valid, do not dictate every future interaction. Start small by sharing something personal but not overwhelming with someone you trust. Notice and reflect on the experience: How did it feel? How was it received? This practice builds confidence in your ability to be vulnerable and helps rewrite the narrative that vulnerability always leads to pain.

Additionally, practicing self-compassion is vital. Be kind to yourself if the thought of opening up feels daunting. Self-compassion involves treating yourself with the same kindness and understanding during moments of fear or uncertainty that you would offer to a good friend.

Embracing vulnerability transforms how you relate to others and, importantly, how you view yourself. It shifts your perspective from seeing yourself as someone who must always appear strong and composed to someone strong because of their capacity to embrace and express their emotions. This shift is liberating and transformative, paving the way for more authentic interactions and relationships. As you continue to explore and practice vulnerability, you'll find that it enriches your connections with others and deepens your connection with yourself, fostering a life led with courage, openness, and authenticity.

6.5 Overcoming Fear of Abandonment: A Guided Approach

The fear of abandonment often feels like an invisible thread that tugs at the heart, affecting how you perceive value within your relationships and influencing your interactions. This fear, deeply rooted in the experiences that shaped your early attachments—perhaps moments when you felt left, unsupported, or uncared for—casts long shadows over your adult relationships. Understanding this fear involves more than recognizing its presence; it's about delving into the experiences that planted these seeds of doubt about your worth and reliability of others' affection and commitment.

The impact of abandonment fear is profound. It can lead you to misinterpret a partner's actions and intentions, seeing indifference where there is merely distraction or rejection where there is none. This fear skews your perception of relational dynamics, often compelling you to cling tighter, which paradoxically can push others away, reinforcing the very abandonment you dread. Relationships, under the weight of such fear, can become battlegrounds of insecurity instead of havens of trust and love. Recognizing how these fears distort your relationship landscape is the first step towards untangling yourself from their grip.

Challenging your abandonment fears involves combining cognitive and behavioral strategies to reshape your thought processes and reaction patterns. Cognitive restructuring, a technique used in cognitive-behavioral therapy, is particularly effective. It encourages you to identify and challenge the often-automatic negative thoughts that fuel your fear of abandonment. For instance, if you often think, "If I don't hear from them, it means they don't care," you might challenge this by considering alternative explanations, such as being busy or having personal stressors. This process of questioning and reevaluating your thoughts helps to reduce their emotional intensity, making them less believable and less capable of influencing your actions.

Behaviorally, exposure therapy can be beneficial. It involves gradually and systematically exposing yourself to the fear of being alone or to scenarios that trigger your fear of abandonment in a controlled and manageable way. This might start with spending an afternoon alone and noting the emotions and thoughts it provokes. Over time, increasing the duration or frequency of these periods helps desensitize you to these triggers, reducing the intensity of your fear. This method, combined with support and guidance from a therapist or a supportive network, can significantly diminish the power of abandonment fears.

It is crucial to build a sense of inner security and self-worth independent of external validation. This internal foundation is built through practices that promote self-awareness and self-compassion. Engaging in activities that foster a sense of accomplishment and joy, such as creative hobbies, learning new skills, or volunteering, can enhance self-esteem. These activities provide intrinsic satisfaction and deepen your sense of self-efficacy, anchoring your self-worth in what you do and who you are rather than the presence or approval of others.

Additionally, regular practice of self-compassion exercises can reinforce your internal security. These include meditations focused on self-kindness or journaling about your positive qualities and achievements. By regularly affirming your worth and treating yourself with compassion, you fortify your emotional defenses against the fears of abandonment, making you less reliant on others for your emotional stability and self-value.

Your capacity to seek out and maintain healthy relationships improves as you cultivate this inner strength. Recognizing the characteristics of healthy relationships—such as mutual respect, honesty, and emotional availability—becomes easier when you're not viewing them through a lens clouded by fear of abandonment. You attract and choose partners who respect and enhance your newfound sense of security. These relationships, rooted in mutual trust and respect, reinforce your feelings of worthiness and further diminish your abandonment fears.

By addressing the roots of your fear, challenging the thoughts that fuel it, and building a robust sense of self-worth, you equip yourself with the tools to manage and overcome the fear of abandonment. This approach does not just alter a single aspect of your life; it transforms your entire emotional landscape, opening up new possibilities for love, connection, and personal fulfillment. As you continue applying these strategies, remember that each step forward is a move towards a more secure and confident you, capable of forging relationships that are not only enduring but also deeply fulfilling.

6.6 Celebrating Progress: Recognizing and Rewarding Your Growth

When you embark on a path toward emotional resilience and secure attachment, one of the most affirming actions you can take is acknowledging and celebrating each step forward, no matter how small. Think of your progress like a garden you've lovingly tended—each new bloom, a victory of persistence and care, deserves recognition. Tracking your progress is not just about recognizing achievements but understanding the depth of your growth and seeing clearly how each challenge faced and obstacle overcome has contributed to a stronger, more resilient you.

Incorporating tracking into your routine can be transformative. It provides tangible evidence of your development and can be an incredible source of motivation. Start with simple methods like keeping a journal or using an app to track personal goals. Document not just milestones but also the subtle shifts in your thoughts and feelings. Perhaps you've noticed a decrease in anxiety in situations that would have previously overwhelmed you, or maybe you're initiating conversations about your needs more openly. These are significant indicators of your growth. Over time, reviewing these entries allows you to see not just where you were but how far you've come, illuminating the path that lies ahead with hope and clarity.

Acknowledging and celebrating this growth involves more than a nod to your progress; it's about creating moments of accurate recognition and joy. Cultivate rituals that honor your achievements. This might look like a small celebration when you reach a goal, indulge in a favorite activity, or purchase something special that reminds you of your journey. You might also share these achievements with a trusted friend or support group, amplifying the joy and reinforcing the significance of your progress. These celebrations act as powerful affirmations, embedding the belief in your abilities and worth and strengthening your commitment to continue.

Adjusting your expectations about growth is also crucial. It's natural to hope for a straight path to improvement, but the reality is often more complex. Growth is non-linear, marked by periods of rapid gains and frustrating plateaus or even temporary setbacks. Embracing this nonlinear nature of growth helps you stay resilient during slower periods. Instead of viewing them as failures, see them as opportunities to consolidate your gains, practice patience, and prepare for the next surge forward. This perspective is more forgiving and accurate—it reflects the true nature of personal development.

Fostering a growth mindset is pivotal in this process. This mindset, centered on the belief that dedication and hard work can develop abilities and intelligence, transforms challenges into learning opportunities rather than mere hurdles. Cultivate this mindset by focusing on what each experience teaches you rather than on a fixed outcome. When a relationship dynamic doesn't change as quickly as you hoped, or when an old anxiety reappears, ask yourself, "What can this teach me?" This approach keeps you open and engaged, ready to extract wisdom from whatever comes your way, ensuring that each step, regardless of direction, adds to your growth.

Embracing these practices of tracking, celebrating, adjusting expectations, and fostering a growth mindset enriches your journey and embeds a more profound sense of self-appreciation and confidence in navigating life's complexities. It's about more than just resilience; it's about recognizing yourself as an active, capable agent in your life, continually evolving and expanding your capacity to love, live fully, and connect deeply.

Reflect on the transformative power of acknowledging your growth as this chapter closes. Each step forward, each moment of resilience, and every instance of vulnerability shared is a testament to your strength and commitment to living a more fulfilled, emotionally rich life. Moving forward, let these celebrations and reflections guide you, providing light and motivation as you continue to navigate your path. Each step, regardless of direction, adds to your growth.

Chapter 7

Integrating New Behaviors and Mindsets

I magine you are embarking on a voyage across a vast ocean. Each day, you chart your course, adjust your sails, and navigate by the stars. This daily commitment to your journey's direction determines not just the speed of your travel but also your success in reaching your destination. Similarly, integrating new behaviors and mindsets into your life, especially those that foster secure attachments, is akin to this daily navigation. It requires consistent effort, a clear direction, and the flexibility to adjust as you learn more about the intricate waters of your emotional landscape.

7.1 Daily Habits for Sustaining Secure Attachments

Routine Building: The importance of daily routines in reinforcing behaviors that contribute to secure attachments.

The power of routine in our lives cannot be overstated. Establishing and adhering to a daily routine can significantly reinforce the behaviors that contribute to secure attachments. Think of your routine as the compass that keeps you oriented towards your emotional goals. It provides structure and predictability, which are crucial not just for managing day-to-day tasks but also for creating an environment where secure attachments can thrive. For example, setting aside time each morning to reflect on your emotional state and intentions for the day can help you remain centered and connected to your relationship goals. This might involve a few minutes of meditation, journaling, or simply setting intentions in front of a mirror. Over time, these moments accumulate, building a foundation of self-awareness and intentionality that supports healthier interactions with others.

Consistency Is Key: How consistency in actions and responses fosters trust and security in relationships.

Consistency is the thread that weaves through the fabric of trust in any relationship. When your actions and responses are consistent, they build a sense of reliability and safety that is fundamental to secure attachments. This doesn't mean you must be perfect; rather, it's about being dependable and coherent in your interactions. For instance, if you commit to being more open in communicating your feelings, let this be evident in your regular interactions. Let your partner, friends, or family members see that they can count on you to express your thoughts and feelings openly, regardless of the situation. This consistency not only strengthens your relationships but also reinforces your own commitment to your new, healthier attachment behaviors, making them more ingrained and natural over time.

Habit Stacking for Attachment: Add small attachment-strengthening activities to existing routines.

Habit stacking is a powerful strategy to incorporate new behaviors into your life without feeling overwhelmed. It involves linking a new habit that promotes secure attachment to an existing routine. For example, if you already have a habit of drinking coffee every morning, you could stack a new habit of sending a caring message or affirmation to your partner or a friend during this time. This method helps you associate the new behavior with an already established routine, increasing the likelihood of the habit sticking. Over time, these small, consistent actions accumulate, significantly enhancing the security and depth of your relationships.

Reflection and Adjustment: Reflect regularly on the effectiveness of these habits and be willing to adjust as needed.

As you integrate new behaviors into your life, regular reflection is crucial. This can be done weekly or monthly and involves looking back at your actions and their outcomes. Ask yourself: Are my new habits helping me foster the kind of relationships I desire? Am I feeling more secure and connected? This reflection is not about critiquing yourself harshly but about assessing and adjusting your course. Perhaps you find that some habits aren't working as well as you hoped, or maybe life's circumstances have changed, requiring a different approach. Adjustments might be necessary, and that's perfectly okay—it's a part of the process. This flexible, reflective approach ensures that your actions continue to align with your ultimate goal of building and sustaining secure, healthy attachments.

7.2 Mindfulness Practices for Relationship Health

Mindful Listening: The role of mindful listening in understanding and connecting with partners.

In the tapestry of relationships, each thread is woven with words, emotions, and silences. Mindful listening is about attending to these threads with the entirety of your presence, tuning into not just what is said, but how it is said, and what is left unspoken. This form of listening transcends the ordinary—it is an active, engaged, and compassionate practice that allows you to truly hear the fears, joys, and underlying needs of your partner. Imagine sitting quietly with your partner, the world's noise faded into the background, your entire focus on their words and emotions. This is where deep connection begins. Mindful listening involves putting aside your own agenda, judgments, and the urge to respond with advice or an anecdote, and instead, giving space to your partner's experiences and emotions. This space, often filled with vulnerability, is where trust deepens and bonds strengthen. It's about hearing the worries behind their words, the love in their laughter, and the unsaid in their silences. By practicing mindful listening, you create a safe, supportive environment, encouraging openness and honesty in your relationship. This doesn't require grand gestures but simply a consistent willingness to be fully present, showing your partner that their thoughts and feelings are valued and important.

Mindful Response: How to respond to partners mindfully, reducing knee-jerk reactions and promoting thoughtful communication.

Responding mindfully in conversations is a powerful extension of mindful listening. It involves processing what your partner has shared and responding in a way that acknowledges their feelings and contributes positively to the dialogue. This practice can transform typical interactions, turning them into opportunities for growth and connection. Consider a situation where your partner expresses disappointment over something you've done. The instinct might be to defend yourself or withdraw, actions often driven by hurt or the fear of criticism. However, a mindful response would be to acknowledge their feelings first, such as saying, "I see you're really upset about this, and I understand why." This acknowledgment doesn't imply agreement or admission of fault, but it shows you are attuned to their feelings. Following this, you can express your perspective without negating theirs. This approach fosters a conversation where both partners feel heard and respected, significantly reducing conflicts and misunderstandings. Mindful responding requires a pause between listening and reacting, a moment where you choose a response that aligns with the values of respect and empathy, rather than reacting out of habit or emotion.

Mindfulness in Conflict: Using mindfulness to stay grounded during relationship conflicts, leading to healthier resolutions.

Conflicts, while challenging, are not inherently detrimental. They can be conduits for deeper understanding and relational growth if navigated with mindfulness. Staying grounded during a conflict means maintaining a connection with your present emotional and physical state, recognizing your feelings without allowing them to dictate your actions. It's about observing the conflict from a place of calm and clarity, rather than from a storm of emotional reactivity. When you feel the surge of anger or frustration, mindfulness encourages you to note these emotions, breathe through them, and respond from a place of composure. This might mean taking deep breaths to calm your heart rate, reminding yourself of your commitment to handle conflicts with care, or even requesting a short break if the emotional intensity becomes overwhelming. Such practices prevent the escalation of conflict and open up a space where both partners can express their concerns without fear of emotional retaliation. The goal is not to avoid conflict but to engage with it constructively, ensuring that it leads to solutions and mutual understanding rather than resentment and distance.

Daily Mindfulness Rituals: Incorporating mindfulness rituals into daily life to enhance presence and connection in relationships.

Incorporating mindfulness into your daily routine can profoundly impact your relationship health. These rituals, ranging from the simple to the structured, help cultivate a habit of presence that extends into your interactions with your partner. Begin by integrating short mindfulness exercises into your daily activities. For example, practice a minute of mindful breathing every morning before you start your day or during the evening when you transition from work to home life. These moments of mindfulness can also be shared with your partner, perhaps starting the day with a short meditation together or sharing a mindful walk, fully present with each other and the environment. Another ritual could involve ending the day by sharing three things you each appreciated about the other that day, a practice that not only fosters mindfulness but also strengthens the emotional bond. Over time, these rituals become woven into the fabric of your relationship, enhancing emotional intimacy and ensuring that mindfulness is not just a tool for conflict resolution but a foundational aspect of your daily interactions.

7.3 The Role of Gratitude in Transforming Attachment Styles

Cultivating a Gratitude Practice

Imagine starting your day not with a checklist of tasks or worries but with a moment of gratitude. This simple shift in focus can profoundly impact your mental and emotional well-being. Gratitude, the art of recognizing and appreciating the positive aspects of life, can significantly alter how you perceive your day and, ultimately, how you engage in your relationships. To cultivate a daily gratitude practice, begin by setting aside a few minutes each morning to reflect on things you are grateful for. It could be as simple as a warm cup of coffee, a text from a friend, or the comfort of your home. Over time, this practice helps rewire your brain to notice positives more readily, fostering a sense of contentment and reducing the tendency to dwell on negative aspects or fears that often accompany anxious attachment. Additionally, consider incorporating gratitude into your regular meditation or mindfulness sessions, using this time to focus on feelings of thankfulness for the relationships and love you have in your life. This regular acknowledgment of the good not only enhances your mood but also shifts your interactions from a place of lack to one of abundance, making you more receptive and appreciative of your connections with others.

Gratitude and Attachment

Gratitude has a unique power to shift the focus from what is lacking in our lives and relationships to what is abundant. For those struggling with anxious attachment, where fear and insecurity often overshadow the joys of connectivity, gratitude can be a transformative tool. By consciously acknowledging the positive attributes your partner brings to your life, or appreciating the moments of connection and joy, you begin to create a buffer against the anxieties that threaten relationship stability. This shift doesn't negate the challenges or dismiss your feelings but provides a more balanced perspective that fosters security and closeness. For example, instead of fixating on a partner's occasional inattentiveness, you might choose to focus on their consistent expressions of care and commitment. This balanced view not only alleviates the pressure created by fear-based narratives but also enhances your capacity to engage in relationships with a sense of security and trust.

Gratitude Journaling for Couples

Sharing a gratitude practice with your partner can significantly strengthen your bond and enhance mutual appreciation. Gratitude journaling for couples is a simple yet powerful way to integrate this practice into your relationship. Set aside a few minutes each week to write down things you are grateful for about each other and the relationship. You can choose to share these lists with each other or keep them private as a personal reminder of your partner's value. This act of writing and reflecting not only deepens your awareness of your partner's positive actions but also promotes a culture of appreciation and kindness within the relationship. Over time, this shared practice can transform the way you see and relate to each other, moving from taking each other's qualities and efforts for granted to celebrating them, thereby fostering a deeper emotional connection and resilience against the typical strains that relationships face.

Overcoming Negativity Bias

Our brains are wired to prioritize negative experiences over positive ones, a trait known as the negativity bias. In the context of relationships, this bias can lead us to overemphasize conflicts or shortcomings, overshadowing the many positive interactions that build attachment and trust. Gratitude directly challenges this bias by refocusing our attention on the positive, which can be especially trans-formative for those with anxious attachment styles, who may be prone to focus-ing on potential threats to relationship security. Regularly practicing gratitude allows you to notice and appreciate the multitude of positive interactions that often go unrecognized but are critical for deepening trust and affection. Over time, this practice not only diminishes the impact of negative biases but also cultivates a more accurate and affirming perception of your relationship, en-couraging a more balanced emotional response to the complexities of intimacy and connection. By fostering this positive focus, gratitude becomes not just a practice but a pathway to a more fulfilled and secure relational life.

7.4 Letting Go of Perfectionism in Relationships

Perfectionism and Attachment: Explore the link between per-fectionism and anxious attachment, including fear of judgment and rejection.

In the delicate dance of relationships, perfectionism often steps in like an un-invited choreographer, dictating steps that are precise but unnatural, leaving little room for the authentic, spontaneous movements that create true intimacy. Perfectionism, deeply rooted in the fear of judgment and rejection, can lead you to set unreasonably high standards for yourself and your relationships. This relentless pursuit of an ideal can be particularly intensified in those with anxious attachment styles, where there is an underlying fear of not being enough. The constant pressure to perform or to make the relationship flawless exacerbates anxiety, leading to a cycle where mistakes are seen not as normal occurrences but as threats to the relationship's stability. Understanding this link is crucial, as it allows you to see how perfectionism not only strains your relationships but also reinforces the fears at the heart of anxious attachment. By recognizing these patterns, you can begin to dismantle the unrealistic expectations that perfec-tionism imposes, paving the way for more genuine and forgiving interactions.

Embracing Imperfection: Strategies for embracing imperfection in oneself and in partners, promoting acceptance and compassion.

Embracing imperfection is akin to giving yourself and your partner permission to be human—to make mistakes, to have off days, and to have quirks and flaws, all of which are intrinsic parts of being alive. One effective strategy for embracing imperfection is to shift your focus from what is lacking to what is present. This means appreciating your partner's efforts and qualities, even if they don't always meet your ideals. It also involves acknowledging your own efforts, recognizing that your value does not diminish because of imperfections. Practicing self-compassion is vital here; it involves treating yourself with the same kindness and understanding during moments of perceived failure as you would a friend. Additionally, cultivating a mindset of growth rather than a mindset of fixed perfection can transform how you view mistakes—seeing them as opportunities for learning and growth rather than as failures. These shifts in perspective not only reduce the pressure imposed by perfectionism but also foster an environment where both you and your partner can feel safe to be your true selves.

Impact on Relationship Dynamics: How letting go of perfectionism can lead to more relaxed and authentic relationship dynamics.

The impact of shedding perfectionism touches every aspect of a relationship, infusing it with a sense of ease and authenticity previously overshadowed by the strain of unrealistic expectations. Relationships, freed from the tight reins of perfectionism, can breathe, allowing for more natural interactions and deeper connections. Couples find that communication improves significantly when neither partner feels pressured to say exactly the right thing at the right time. This openness paves the way for more honest exchanges, where vulnerabilities can be shared without fear of judgment, deepening the emotional connection. Moreover, letting go of the need to control every aspect of the relationship can lead to a surprising discovery: that the moments of unexpected joy and spontaneity—those that occur precisely because everything isn't controlled or perfect—are often the ones that strengthen the bond the most. This more relaxed dynamic encourages a supportive rather than critical atmosphere, where each partner feels appreciated and valued, not for their ability to meet certain standards, but for their inherent worth.

Practical Exercises: Practical exercises to challenge perfectionist thoughts and behaviors related to attachment and relationships.

Challenging perfectionist thoughts and behaviors can be approached through practical, daily exercises that promote awareness and change. One effective exercise is the "Three C's" practice: Catch, Check, and Change. First, catch yourself in the moment of a perfectionist thought or behavior. This might be a thought like, "I need to always have the perfect response," or a behavior like redoing a task you've already completed because it wasn't perfect the first time. Second, check the thought or behavior by asking yourself whether it's realistic or necessary, and what it costs you emotionally. Finally, change the thought or behavior by replacing it with a more forgiving and realistic approach. For example, instead of redoing the task, you might decide it's good enough as it is, or instead of searching for the perfect response, you might speak from the heart without overthinking. Another useful exercise involves setting "good enough" goals. These are tasks or objectives set with the intention of doing them well enough, rather than perfectly. This practice helps break the habit of striving for perfection, promoting a healthier, more balanced approach to tasks and interactions. Regularly engaging in these exercises not only helps reduce perfectionist tendencies but also enhances your ability to enjoy more relaxed and authentic relationships, free from the constraints of unrealistic expectations.

7.5 The Power of Positive Affirmations in Attachment Recovery

Creating Affirmations

Imagine transforming your inner dialogue into a nurturing voice, one that supports and uplifts you as you navigate the complexities of relationships and self-perception. This transformation is at the heart of creating personal affirmations, powerful statements that can reshape your thoughts and propel you toward a more secure attachment style. Affirmations are tailored declarations that counteract deeply ingrained fears and insecurities, replacing them with empowering beliefs and self-acceptance. To craft affirmations that resonate with your specific emotional needs, start by identifying the negative beliefs that often surface in your relationships. These might be thoughts like "I am too much for anyone to handle" or "I am always going to be abandoned." Reflect on these statements and ask yourself what you wish you could believe instead. From this reflection, formulate affirmations that directly address these insecurities. For example, "I am worthy of love and respect," or "I am capable of maintaining healthy, lasting relationships." These affirmations should be positive, in the present tense, and expressed as if they are already true. By doing this, you're not just hoping for a future change; you're beginning to embody this change in your current self-perception.

Incorporating Affirmations

To integrate these powerful affirmations into your daily life, consider their placement within your routine where they will have the most impact. One effective method is to begin your day with your affirmations, setting a tone of self-empowerment from the moment you wake. You might place sticky notes with your affirmations on your bathroom mirror or fridge, or set them as reminders on your phone to pop up throughout the day. Another impactful approach is to incorporate them into your self-care practices, such as saying them aloud during a morning yoga session or while meditating. This repeated vocal affirmation reinforces their power, embedding these positive beliefs deeper into your subconscious. Over time, these affirmations become more than just words; they start to manifest in your actions and interactions, significantly altering how you perceive and engage with the world around you. By consistently affirming your worth and capabilities, you build a foundation of self-esteem that supports healthier, more secure attachments.

Affirmations and Self-Worth

The role of affirmations extends beyond altering specific behaviors or thoughts; they are pivotal in enhancing overall self-worth. For those dealing with anxious attachment, where self-doubt and dependency on external validation can be prevalent, affirmations serve as reminders of your intrinsic worth, independent of any relationship. This practice fosters a sense of internal security that diminishes the need for external approval to feel valued and loved. As you repeat affirmations like "I am complete on my own" or "My value doesn't decrease based on someone's inability to see my worth," you start to dissociate your self-esteem from your relationship status or partner's actions. This detachment is crucial in developing healthier relationships where your well-being does not hinge on another's presence or mood but is grounded in a stable, self-affirmed identity.

Measuring Impact

To truly appreciate the impact of affirmations on your attachment style and relationships, regular reflection is essential. Take time each week to reflect on how your affirmations are influencing your thoughts and interactions. Notice any shifts in your dialogue with yourself and with others. Are you feeling more empowered to express your needs? Do you find yourself less reactive to perceived slights or withdrawals? Observing these changes can provide tangible proof of the positive shifts occurring, reinforcing your commitment to this practice.

Additionally, you might find it helpful to journal about your experiences with affirmations, noting any changes in your emotional responses or relationship dynamics. This written record not only tracks your progress but also reinforces the effectiveness of your affirmations, encouraging you to continue this beneficial practice. As you witness the transformative power of affirmations in your life, they become not just phrases you say but truths you live by, fundamentally enhancing your sense of self and enriching your relationships.

7.6 Cultivating Joy and Playfulness in Adult Relationships

Embracing joy and playfulness within your relationships acts as a refreshing breeze that can invigorate and enrich your connections. In our adult lives, burdened with responsibilities and often overshadowed by the seriousness of daily tasks, we might forget how vital it is to infuse our interactions with lightness and fun. This playful energy is essential, not just for maintaining a healthy, vibrant relationship but also for nurturing a living environment where love thrives on laughter and mutual joy.

Consider playfulness as a nutrient for your relationship's growth, essential as the sunlight that warms your face or the water that quenches your thirst. It is a powerful antidote to the routine and stress that often seep into our interactions, making them feel more like transactions than exchanges of affection. Engaging in playful activities together can significantly strengthen your bond. Simple joys like dancing in your living room, cooking a spontaneous and exotic dinner together, or even playing board games can ignite joy and laughter, drawing you closer. These activities encourage you to step out of your usual roles and responsibilities and connect at a momentary level that is free from the burden of adult expectations. They remind you of the joyous aspects of your partnership, reinforcing the foundations of your emotional connection.

However, barriers to playfulness, such as stress, routine, and past traumas, can dampen this joyful spirit. Stress, often a constant in our hurried lives, can make us too tired or distracted to engage in play. Routine, while providing a necessary structure, can also render our interactions predictable and uninspiring. Meanwhile, unresolved traumas from past relationships may cause us to guard ourselves against the vulnerability that playfulness can entail. Recognizing these barriers is the first step towards mitigating their effects. Addressing stress through mindfulness or physical activities, breaking the monotony of routine with spontaneous adventures, and healing past traumas through therapy or self-reflection can reopen doors to a playful engagement with life and love.

Playfulness also serves as a pathway to developing secure attachments. It creates an atmosphere of trust and safety, where you can express yourselves freely and creatively without fear of judgment. In moments of play, you often reveal your most unguarded selves, learning to trust not only in each other's good intentions but also in the strength of your bond. When you laugh together, you are building a reservoir of goodwill and positive memories that can buffer against future conflicts or misunderstandings, reinforcing the resilience of your relationship.

Incorporating regular playful interactions into your relationship can transform the dynamic between you and your partner, making the relationship feel more alive and dynamic. These moments of shared joy not only enhance your immediate happiness but also deepen your connection, ensuring that your relationship continues to grow and flourish, filled with laughter and lightness that carry you through the tougher moments. By fostering this playful spirit, you not only enjoy each other's company more but also cultivate a relationship that is rich in joy and satisfaction, making every day together an opportunity to celebrate your bond.

In embracing the joy and playfulness of your relationship, you witness a delightful transformation not only in how you interact with your partner but also in how you view the world around you. This chapter has explored how integrating playfulness can significantly enhance the quality of your relationships and contribute to a secure and joyful connection. As we continue to weave these themes into the fabric of our lives, we open ourselves to a richer, more fulfilling experience of love and companionship. As this chapter closes, let the ideas resonate and inspire you to infuse more playful moments into your relationships, nurturing a joyful, vibrant connection that uplifts and sustains both you and your partner.

Chapter 8

Building Community and Support

In the tapestry of our lives, each thread represents the connections we weave with others—each one vital, each one a potential source of strength and healing. Imagine, for a moment, a single thread trying to hold up against the pull of everyday challenges. It stands a better chance of holding strong when supported by many threads, intricately woven into a resilient fabric. This metaphor beautifully encapsulates the essence of building community and support systems in our lives, especially when navigating the complexities of anxious attachment. The truth is, healing often happens in the company of others who provide empathy, understanding, and shared experiences.

8.1 Finding Your Tribe: Building Support Systems for Healing

Community Importance

The journey to overcoming anxious attachment and fostering secure relationships can sometimes feel lonely, but it needn't be a solitary path. Finding a supportive community is akin to finding a harbor in a storm—providing a safe place to anchor, share burdens, and find rest. The importance of such a community lies not only in the practical support it offers but also in the emotional resonance and understanding you find among those who have walked similar paths. These connections can validate your feelings and experiences, significantly alleviating the isolation that often accompanies mental health struggles. In these spaces, shared vulnerabilities become strengths, as each member's journey contributes to a collective wisdom that no one person could achieve alone.

Seeking Like-Minded Individuals

Building your tribe involves seeking out individuals or groups who not only share your experiences but also your hopes and aspirations for healing and growth. Start by identifying what you need most in your support network. Are you looking for empathy, motivation, accountability, or perhaps all three? Places to look include local support groups, workshops focused on mental health and attachment, or even online platforms dedicated to emotional wellness. Engaging in activities that align with your interests can also naturally lead to connections with like-minded individuals. Whether it's a yoga class, an art therapy session, or a book club, these settings provide a backdrop for conversations that can forge meaningful relationships centered around mutual support and personal growth.

Online and Offline Communities

Both online and offline communities have unique benefits in building and maintaining support systems. Offline, local communities offer a tangible sense of presence and immediacy that can be incredibly comforting—there's undeniable power in physically sitting with others who understand your struggles. Activities like group therapy or local meetups allow for real-time interaction and the development of deep, personal connections. Online communities, on the other hand, offer accessibility and anonymity, which can be particularly appealing if you're just beginning to reach out or if you live in an area where local resources are scarce. Platforms like forums, social media groups, and dedicated mental health networks enable you to connect with a vast network of individuals who share your experiences and offer support at any time of the day, transcending geographical limitations.

Creating Safe Spaces

Whether online or in person, the effectiveness of these communities largely depends on their ability to foster open, supportive interactions. Creating a safe space requires clear boundaries and a shared commitment to respect and confidentiality. If you're leading a group, set ground rules that encourage open dialogue while safeguarding personal dignity and privacy. Encourage an atmosphere where members feel comfortable sharing their fears and triumphs without fear of judgment. In online settings, moderating discussions to keep them respectful and on-topic can help maintain a supportive environment. Additionally, being proactive in expressing appreciation for each member's contributions can cultivate a positive group dynamic that encourages ongoing participation and support.

Engaging with your community, whether seeking one out or nurturing one, is not a passive experience. It requires intentionality, vulnerability, and a willingness to both give and receive support. As you weave these new threads into the fabric of your life, you strengthen not only your resilience and capacity for joy but also your ability to forge deeper, more meaningful connections. As you continue to weave these connections, remember that each interaction, each shared story, and each moment of support adds to the rich, supportive network that surrounds you, bolstering you against the challenges and enriching your journey towards healing and growth.

8.2 When to Seek Professional Help: A Guide to Therapeutic Support

In the quiet moments of reflection, you might find yourself facing emotions and memories that are hard to untangle alone. Recognizing when you need professional help is a profound step towards healing—not a sign of weakness, but of courage and self-awareness. Many people grapple with the decision to seek therapy, especially when dealing with anxious attachment, because the symptoms—constant worry about relationships, fear of rejection, and emotional highs and lows—can often be dismissed as just being part of who they are. However, when these patterns start to significantly impact your daily life, relationships, and happiness, it's important to acknowledge that professional help can offer new insights and strategies for change.

Recognizing the need for therapy often comes from a place of feeling stuck or noticing that despite your best efforts, you're not making the progress you hoped for. It might manifest as a pervasive sadness, an unshakeable anxiety, or relationships that consistently feel strained or unfulfilling despite your best efforts. Other signs include reactions that feel disproportionate to their triggers, or emotional responses that seem automatic and difficult to control. These experiences can be indicators that underlying issues, perhaps rooted deep in your past or in subconscious beliefs about self-worth and attachment, need to be addressed with the help of a professional.

Finding the right therapist is crucial and can feel daunting, but it's a process worth investing your time and heart into. Start by considering what might work best for you in terms of therapeutic approaches—do you think you could benefit from cognitive-behavioral therapy to reshape thought patterns, or perhaps psychodynamic therapy to delve deeper into emotional and relationship patterns? Researching these approaches can help you understand what aligns with your needs. When looking for a therapist, it's essential to consider their qualifications, but equally, their approach to therapy and whether their personality and methods resonate with you. Many therapists offer a consultation call or session, which can be a great opportunity to see if you feel comfortable with them—trust your instincts here. Compatibility plays a significant role in the therapeutic relationship; feeling understood and safe with your therapist is foundational for effective therapy.

Therapy is a powerful tool for growth, particularly for those dealing with anxious attachment. It provides a structured environment to explore your thoughts, feelings, and behaviors in a way that everyday introspection or conversation with friends cannot. With professional guidance, you can identify the roots of your insecure attachment, understand how it's impacting your relationships, and learn healthier ways to connect with others. Therapy offers a blend of challenge and support, pushing you to confront painful truths while providing the tools to heal and transform those pains into sources of strength and insight.

Managing expectations when entering therapy is vital. It's important to understand that therapy is not a quick fix but a gradual process that involves work and commitment, both during sessions and outside of them. The timeline can vary widely depending on individual circumstances and the issues being addressed. Some people see significant changes in a few months, while for others, the process may take longer. It's also a collaborative process—much of the success of therapy depends on your willingness to be open and active in the process. Discussing your goals and expectations with your therapist can help set a clear framework for your sessions and help manage the pace and progress of your therapy. Remember, the goal of therapy is not just to alleviate symptoms but to foster an enduring change that improves your quality of life and relationships.

As you consider the possibility of therapy, remember that it is a sign of strength to ask for help. It reflects a commitment to yourself and your well-being, and while the decision to start can be difficult, the rewards can be transformative, offering a pathway to deeper understanding and more fulfilling relationships.

8.3 Group Therapy and Workshops: Learning and Growing Together

In the realm of healing and personal growth, the shared journey of group therapy and workshops can serve as a beacon of collective strength and wisdom. Imagine a space where you, along with others traversing similar emotional landscapes, come together not just to share your stories but to actively shape your paths to emotional well-being. Group therapy offers a unique environment where the power of shared experiences fosters a deep sense of connection and mutual support, essential elements for anyone working through the intricacies of anxious attachment.

The benefits of group therapy extend far beyond the comfort of knowing you're not alone in your struggles. In these settings, the collective experience of the group can illuminate diverse perspectives and coping strategies that might have remained obscured in individual therapy or personal reflection. Each member's journey enriches the group's understanding, providing multiple vantage points from which to view challenges and successes. This communal learning environment cultivates a rich soil from which new insights and methods can grow, offering you fresh approaches to managing your attachment style and enhancing your relationships. Moreover, witnessing others' progress and resilience can be incredibly empowering, reinforcing your belief in the possibility of change and growth. The group becomes a mirror reflecting the collective strength and potential of its members, including you, reinforcing that recovery and growth are not just possible but are being actively achieved.

Workshops focusing on attachment, relationships, and personal growth provide structured opportunities to delve deeper into specific areas of interest or need. These might range from learning about the psychological theories underpinning attachment styles to practicing communication skills that enhance relationship health. The interactive nature of workshops allows for real-time feedback and skill practice, which is invaluable in solidifying new knowledge and behaviors. For instance, a workshop on effective communication in relationships can transform your understanding of how to express needs and listen empathetically, skills that are crucial for building secure attachments. The facilitators of these workshops often bring specialized knowledge and techniques, providing guidance that is both informed and practical. Participating in these focused sessions can accelerate your learning and application of new strategies, making them powerful adjuncts to your overall growth plan.

Active participation in group therapy and workshops is key to maximizing their benefits. Engaging fully not only enhances your own learning but also contributes to the group's dynamic. Sharing your experiences openly and offering feedback to others not only helps in cementing your own insights but also supports fellow participants in their growth. This reciprocity of support and learning is what makes group settings profoundly effective. It's important to approach each session as an opportunity to both teach and learn, to give and receive. This active engagement helps transform theoretical knowledge into practical wisdom, embedding new understanding into your daily life and inter-actions.

Safety and confidentiality are pillars that uphold the integrity and effectiveness of group therapy and workshops. These settings often establish strict norms to ensure that every participant can share openly without fear of judgment or breach of privacy. Facilitators typically set clear guidelines about confidentiality and respectful communication at the outset, creating a secure framework within which all discussions take place. Understanding these guidelines and committing to uphold them enhances the safety of the space for everyone involved. This commitment to confidentiality and respect is crucial in fostering an atmosphere where vulnerability is not just possible but is protected and valued, enabling all members to explore and share their deepest fears and hopes in a supportive environment.

Engaging in group therapy and workshops can significantly enrich your healing process, providing you with a spectrum of perspectives and a community of support. These experiences remind you that while your path to greater emotional health is personal, it need not be lonely. The collective wisdom and encouragement found in these settings reinforce your resilience and expand your toolkit for managing relationships, turning the journey into a shared adventure in growth and healing.

8.4 Navigating the Therapeutic Relationship: Tips for Success

Embarking on therapy can often feel like stepping into a delicately balanced dance where each step, each turn holds the potential for profound self-discovery and healing. Central to this therapeutic dance is the relationship you cultivate with your therapist—a dynamic built on trust, openness, and mutual respect. The strength of this relationship is not merely a byproduct of effective therapy; rather, it is the bedrock upon which the process of healing is built. Imagine entering a space where you feel wholly seen, heard, and supported, where the weight of judgment is lifted, and the freedom to explore the deepest corners of your psyche is granted. This is the essence of a strong therapeutic alliance, and it is crucial for navigating the complexities of anxious attachment and other deep-seated emotional issues.

Building this alliance begins with trust, which is both a starting point and an ongoing process. Trust in a therapeutic setting is cultivated through consistent experiences of the therapist's empathy, confidentiality, and professional competence. It's about feeling confident that your therapist not only understands your concerns but also respects your boundaries and is committed to your well-being. This trust enables you to venture into vulnerable territories in your psyche and relationships, areas you might have walled off due to past hurts or fears. A therapist who responds to your disclosures with sensitivity and insight can transform the therapeutic space into a secure base from which you can explore and grow. As you share more and experience the therapist's non-judgmental support, your trust deepens, further solidifying this foundational aspect of your therapeutic relationship.

Openness and honesty are the twin pillars that support this evolving relationship. Therapy is most effective when you can be wholly transparent about your thoughts, feelings, and behaviors. This level of honesty can be daunting, especially when it involves expressing painful or embarrassing truths. However, the therapeutic environment is designed to be a safe space where such disclosures are not only protected but are also essential for healing. Your therapist can only guide you effectively if they fully understand the challenges you are facing. This openness requires courage, and it's important to pace yourself; share at a level that feels manageable as you gradually build comfort with being more open. Remember, your therapist is there to support you, not to pass judgment or push you beyond what you're ready to handle.

Feedback and adjustments form another critical aspect of navigating your therapeutic relationship. Therapy is not a one-size-fits-all process, and what works for one person may not work for another. It's important to regularly reflect on how you feel the therapy is progressing and to communicate this with your therapist. If certain approaches or discussions make you uncomfortable or don't seem to be helping, it's okay to speak up about these feelings. A good therapist will welcome your feedback and be willing to adjust their methods to better suit your needs. This might mean trying different therapeutic techniques, adjusting the focus of your sessions, or even revisiting the goals of your therapy. This kind of collaborative approach not only ensures that your therapy aligns with your evolving needs but also empowers you as an active participant in your healing process.

Understanding the role of the therapist as a secure base can profoundly impact your therapeutic journey. In the context of anxious attachment, where fears of instability and abandonment can dominate, a therapist often embodies the role of a secure, reliable presence. This relationship model provides a corrective emotional experience, especially if your past relationships have been unstable or if your attachment needs have been inconsistently met. Over time, this therapeutic relationship can teach you what a secure attachment feels like, helping you internalize these experiences and apply them to other relationships in your life. The consistency and reliability of your therapist provide a framework within which you can explore your fears and learn new, healthier ways of relating to others and to yourself.

As you navigate your therapeutic relationship, remember that this is your space to heal, learn, and grow. The dynamics of this relationship—built on trust, openness, and mutual respect—can provide a powerful model for forming secure attachments outside of therapy, enriching your relationships and enhancing your overall quality of life.

8.5 Online Resources and Communities for Anxious Attachment

In today's digital age, the internet has become a pivotal ally in the quest for mental health support, offering a vast ocean of resources that can be both enlightening and overwhelming. When you begin to explore online resources for anxious attachment and recovery, the key lies in navigating this vastness with discernment and purpose. Start by identifying your specific needs—whether seeking understanding, learning coping strategies, or finding community support. Websites, blogs, and scholarly articles can provide a wealth of information that helps deepen your understanding of anxious attachment. Look for sources that cite reputable research or are written by professionals in the field of psychology and mental health. Evaluating the credibility of online content is crucial; check the qualifications of the authors and the quality of the sources cited to ensure the information is reliable and based on sound research.

Participating in online forums and support groups can be a transformative experience, offering a sense of community and shared understanding that is hard to replicate in other formats. These platforms allow you to connect with individuals from around the globe who share similar experiences and challenges. The benefits of such interactions not only provide emotional support and validation, but they also offer practical advice and insights that can be invaluable in your recovery process. However, it's important to approach online forums with caution. The anonymity of the internet can sometimes lead to unmoderated discussions that may not always be constructive. Choose forums that have active moderators and clear rules about respectful and supportive interactions. Participate actively but protectively, sharing your experiences while maintaining boundaries that preserve your emotional safety.

The digital era also brings the power of specialized tools and apps designed to support mental health and foster recovery from anxious attachment. Many of these digital tools offer guided exercises, tracking capabilities, and personalized feedback that can help you manage anxiety, enhance self-awareness, and build healthier relationship patterns. Apps that focus on mindfulness and meditation can be particularly helpful, as they provide techniques to calm the mind and center the emotions, which are essential skills for anyone dealing with anxious attachment. Additionally, some apps are designed specifically to help you understand and improve your attachment style through interactive content and daily prompts that encourage reflection and growth. When selecting digital tools and apps, look for ones that prioritize user privacy and data security. Read reviews and check their privacy policies to ensure your information is protected.

Maintaining privacy and safety online is paramount, especially when dealing with sensitive issues like mental health. As you engage with online communities and resources, be mindful of the information you share. Protect your identity and personal details, especially in public forums or groups. Use secure passwords, and be cautious about clicking on links that could lead to insecure websites or downloads that may contain malware. If an online interaction ever makes you feel uncomfortable or unsafe, trust your instincts and disengage. Remember, the goal of using these online resources is to support your healing and growth; it's important to do so in a way that also protects your well-being and privacy.

Navigating online resources effectively requires a balance of openness and caution, engagement and discernment. By carefully selecting and utilizing these digital avenues, you can greatly enrich your understanding of anxious attachment and find meaningful support that enhances your journey toward recovery. As you continue to explore the vast resources available online, let them serve as tools that empower you to understand more deeply, connect more authentically, and grow more confidently into the secure, fulfilled individual you are capable of becoming.

8.6 Creating a Personalized Recovery Map: Integrating All You've Learned

In the process of healing and growth, having a clear and personalized recovery map can serve as your compass, guiding you through the complexities of emotional recovery and towards a life of healthier attachments. Think of this map as a living document, one that not only charts where you are and where you want to go but also grows and adapts with you through your recovery process. It's about weaving together everything you've learned about yourself, your relationships, and your needs into a cohesive, actionable plan.

The creation of your recovery map starts with a clear understanding of your current state and an envisioning of where you aim to be. This might include being more securely attached in relationships, feeling less anxiety about abandonment, or being able to express your needs and emotions more clearly. From here, setting concrete, achievable milestones is crucial. These are not just goals but signposts that mark your progress as you move forward. For instance, a milestone could be recognizing and responding differently to a trigger that would have previously led you into a spiral of anxiety. Another might be having a difficult conversation with a partner or friend without feeling overwhelmed.

These milestones should reflect both your growth in self-awareness and your ability to apply new strategies in real-life scenarios.

Incorporating your support systems into your recovery map is essential. This means identifying who in your life can provide emotional support, practical advice, or simply a listening ear when needed. Friends, family members, therapists, or even members of a support group can all be part of this network. However, it's important to choose people who are not only trustworthy but also understand your goals and are committed to supporting you in a way that respects your boundaries and needs. Outline how and when you might reach out to these individuals for support. For instance, you might decide to check in with a close friend once a week or schedule regular sessions with your therapist. These check-ins can provide you with valuable feedback and encouragement, helping you stay aligned with your recovery goals.

Regular review and adaptation of your recovery map are what make it a truly effective tool. As you grow and your circumstances change, your needs and goals might also evolve. Perhaps a milestone that once seemed crucial no longer aligns with your priorities, or a new challenge emerges that requires you to adjust your strategies. Set a regular schedule to review your map—this could be monthly or quarterly—reflecting on what's working, what isn't, and what might need to change. This ongoing process not only ensures that your recovery map remains relevant but also reinforces your commitment to your growth and adaptation over time. It's a practice in mindfulness and proactive adjustment, keeping you deeply connected to your journey of healing.

By taking the time to develop a personalized recovery map, you empower yourself with a clear direction and structured plan that guides your healing process. This map is not just a set of directions but a reflection of your commitment to yourself and your future—a future where you feel more secure, understood, and connected in your relationships. As you continue to update and refine your map, it becomes a dynamic testament to your resilience and ability to navigate the path to emotional well-being.

As this chapter wraps up, we reflect on the importance of a personalized recovery map in guiding your path through healing and growth. By setting clear milestones, integrating support systems, and regularly updating your plan, you equip yourself with the tools needed to navigate the complexities of recovery with confidence and clarity. This map is not just a plan but a living document that grows with you, adapting to your evolving needs and helping you stay aligned with your ultimate goals of emotional health and secure attachments. As we turn the page, we carry forward the insights and strategies that have shaped your recovery map, ready to explore further dimensions of healing and growth.

Spreading the Love

Now that you have learned about healing anxious attachment and securing lasting relationships, it's time to pass on your newfound knowledge and show other readers where they can find the same help.

Your journey through "Compassionate Strategies for Anxious Attachment Recovery" has given you tools to overcome your fears and build stronger, more secure connections. Imagine how many others could benefit from these insights!

If this book has made a difference in your life, consider leaving a review. Your thoughts and experiences could be the guiding light for someone else seeking help.

Here's why your review matters:

- **It offers hope:** Your story can inspire others to start their own healing journey.

- **It provides guidance:** Sharing how the book helped you can show others the practical benefits they can gain.

- **It builds a community:** Your review helps create a supportive space for everyone dealing with anxious attachment.

To spread the love and help others find this resource, leave a review. It takes just a moment, but its impact can last a lifetime.

Simply scan the QR code below to leave your review:

Thank you for being part of this journey and for helping others find their path to healing and secure relationships.

- Take Care, Anne Moigis

Conclusion

A s we draw this journey to a close, I want to take a moment to reflect on the transformative path we've navigated together—from grappling with the roots of anxious attachment, through the deep waters of healing trauma, to the shores of forming secure and resilient relationships. We've explored the intricate dance of understanding our attachment styles, the profound impact of both Big T and little t traumas, and the empowering steps toward building emotional resilience and secure connections.

Healing and fostering secure attachments is undeniably a journey that requires patience, kindness towards oneself, and an enduring commitment to growth. It's important to remember that this process isn't linear and each step forward is a victory. Embrace self-compassion, for it is your gentle companion in times of challenge and change.

In our discussions, the significant role of therapy, particularly EMDR, emerged as a cornerstone for those struggling with the shadows of past traumas. EMDR therapy offers a beacon of hope, helping to process these deep-rooted pains and fostering a move towards secure attachment. If you find yourself resonating with this approach, I encourage you to seek a certified EMDR therapist who can guide you through this healing process.

The journey towards overcoming anxious attachment is an ongoing process of self-discovery and nurturing. Continue to engage in self-reflection, embrace the practices of mindfulness, reconnect with your inner child, and set boundaries that honor your wellbeing. Communication and trust are the pillars upon which secure relationships are built. Remember, every effort you put into these areas propels you towards a more secure and fulfilling connection with yourself and others.

I urge you to not walk this path alone. Building or joining a supportive community can tremendously amplify your healing process. Whether these connections are forged face-to-face, or span across digital landscapes, they are invaluable. They provide not just solace but also perspectives that can catalyze your growth.

Now, I invite you to take that brave first step towards change. Whether it's reaching out for professional help, practicing the strategies outlined in our chapters, or simply sharing your story with a trusted friend, each step is a move towards a more secure and joyful you.

As we part ways in this book, I am filled with hope for you. Change is not only possible; it is within your reach. You possess the innate strength and resilience required to cultivate lasting and secure relationships. Thank you deeply for allowing me to be a part of your journey to healing and growth. May you carry forward this spirit of courage and compassion, and may it light your path to deeper connections and self-realization.

References

1. Healthline. (n.d.). Anxious attachment: Signs in children and adults, causes, and more. Healthline. Retrieved June 11, 2024, from https://www.healthline.com/health/mental-health/anxious-attachment

2. Vasileva, M., & Petermann, F. (2017). Manifestation of trauma: The effect of early traumatic experiences on the emotional and cognitive functioning of children. *Frontiers in Psychology*, *8*, 5364177. https://www.ncbi.nlm.nih.gov/pmc/articles/PMC5364177/

3. Zhang, X., Li, T., & Li, X. (2021). Anxious attachment is associated with heightened activation of brain regions involved in social pain and emotion regulation. *Journal of Psychiatric Research*, *133*, 20-27. https://www.sciencedirect.com/science/article/pii/S2213158821000292

4. Highland Park Therapy. (2024, March 30). Healing attachment trauma through attachment-focused EMDR. Highland Park . https://www.highlandparktherapy.com/blog/2024/3/30/healing-attachment-trauma-through-attachment-focused-emdr#:~:text=Research%20has%20shown%20promising%20results,functioning%20and%20quality%20of%20life.

5. JourneyPure. (n.d.). What's the difference between big "T" and little "t" trauma? JourneyPure River. Retrieved June 11, 2024, from https://journeypureriver.com/big-t-little-t-trauma/

6. Rodgers Counseling. (n.d.). EMDR and attachment trauma. Rodgers Counseling. Retrieved June 11, 2024, from https://rodgerscounseli ng.com/emdr-and-attachment-trauma/

7. Verywell Mind. (n.d.). How does somatic experiencing therapy work? Verywell Mind. Retrieved June 11, 2024, from https://www.verywe llmind.com/what-is-somatic-experiencing-5204186

8. Fearon, R. M. P., & Belsky, J. (2011). Infant-parent attachment: Definition, types, antecedents, and implications for developmental psychopathology. *Child Development Perspectives*, 5(2), 104-110. https://www.ncbi.nlm.nih.gov/pmc/articles/PMC2724160/

9. Healthline. (n.d.). 14 mindfulness tricks to reduce anxiety. Healthline. Retrieved June 11, 2024, from https://www.healthline.com/health/mindfulness-tricks-to-reduce-anxiety

10. Positive Psychology. (n.d.). Inner child healing: 35 practical tools for growing beyond. Positive Psychology. Retrieved June 11, 2024, from https://positivepsychology.com/inner-child-healing/

11. Liberty Counseling Luxembourg. (n.d.). What is attachment-focused EMDR? Liberty Counseling Luxembourg. Retrieved June 11, 2024, https://libertycounsellingluxembourg.com/attachment-focused-em dr/#:~:text=AF%2DEMDR%20helps%20the%20client,and%20safet y%20in%20the%20client.

12. Mindful. (n.d.). Why self-compassion is essential to healing. Mindful. Retrieved June 11, 2024, from https://www.mindful.org/why-self-c ompassion-is-essential-to-healing/

13. Schwartz, A. (n.d.). Complex PTSD and attachment trauma. Dr. Arielle Schwartz. Retrieved June 11, 2024, from https://drarielleschwartz.com/complex-ptsd-and-attachment-t rauma-dr-arielle-schwartz/

14. HelpGuide. (n.d.). Effective communication: Improving your interpersonal skills. HelpGuide. Retrieved June 11, 2024, from https://www.helpguide.org/articles/relationships-communica tion/effective-communication.htm

15. Highland Park Therapy. (2024, March 30). Healing attachment trauma through attachment-focused EMDR. Highland Park https://www.highlandparktherapy.com/blog/2024/3/30/healing-att achment-trauma-through-attachment-focused-emdr#:~:text=Resear ch%20has%20shown%20promising%20results,functioning%20and% 20quality%20of%20life.

16. MacWilliam, B. (n.d.). How to overcome anxious attachment. Briana MacWilliam. Retrieved June 11, 2024, from https://brianamacwilli am.com/overcome-anxious-attachment/

17. WebMD. (n.d.). Anxious attachment: How to know if you have it. WebMD. Retrieved June 11, 2024, from https://www.webmd.com/mental-health/what-is-anxious-attachmen t#:~:text=People%20with%20this%20attachment%20style,that%20w as%20scary%20and%20traumatizing.

18. Positive Psychology. (n.d.). 24 forgiveness activities, exercises, tips, and worksheets. Positive Psychology. Retrieved June 11, 2024, from https://positivepsychology.com/forgiveness-exercises-tips-acti vities-worksheets/

19. Highland Park Therapy. (2024, March 30). Healing attachment trauma through attachment-focused EMDR. Highland Park https://www.highlandparktherapy.com/blog/2024/3/30/healing-att achment-trauma-through-attachment-focused-emdr#:~:text=Resear ch%20has%20shown%20promising%20results,functioning%20and% 20quality%20of%20life.

20. HelpGuide. (n.d.). Improving emotional intelligence (EQ): Expert

guide. HelpGuide. Retrieved June 11, 2024, from https://www.he lpguide.org/articles/mental-health/emotional-intelligence-eq.htm

21. Healthline. (n.d.). Anxious attachment: Signs in children and adults, causes, and more. Healthline. Retrieved June 11, 2024, from https:/ /www.healthline.com/health/mental-health/anxious-attachment

22. Highland Park Therapy. (2024, March 30). Healing attachment trauma through attachment-focused EMDR. Highland Park https://www.highlandparktherapy.com/blog/2024/3/30/heali ng-attachment-trauma-through-attachment-focused-emdr

23. Positive Psychology. (n.d.). What is emotional resilience? (+6 proven ways to build it). Positive Psychology. Retrieved June 11, 2024, from https://positivepsychology.com/emotional-resilience/

24. Positive Psychology. (n.d.). How to overcome fear of abandonment: 6 helpful tips. Positive Psychology. Retrieved June 11, 2024, from https://positivepsychology.com/fear-of-abandonment/

25. Evergreen Psychotherapy Center. (n.d.). Why are family routines and rituals important for a child with compromised attachment? Evergreen Psychotherapy Center. Retrieved June 11, 2024, from https://evergreenpsychotherapycenter.com/why-are-family-routines -and-rituals-important-for-a-child-with-compromised-attachment/

26. Gottman Institute. (n.d.). How to use mindfulness to strength- en your relationships. Gottman Institute. Retrieved June 11, 2024, from https://www.gottman.com/blog/how-to-use-mindfulness-to -strengthen-your-relationships/

27. Therapist Aid. (n.d.). Couple's gratitude journal | Worksheet. Thera- pist Aid. Retrieved June 11, 2024, from https://www.therapistaid.c om/therapy-worksheet/couples-gratitude-journal

28. Highland Park Therapy. (2024, March 30). Healing attachment

trauma through attachment-focused EMDR. Highland Park https://www.highlandparktherapy.com/blog/2024/3/30/healing-att achment-trauma-through-attachment-focused-emdr#:~:text=Resear ch%20has%20shown%20promising%20results,functioning%20and% 20quality%20of%20life.

29. PsychCentral. (n.d.). Attachment trauma: Effects, examples, and how to heal. PsychCentral. Retrieved June 11, 2024, from https://psychc entral.com/health/attachment-trauma

30. Highland Park Therapy. (2024, March 30). Healing attachment trauma through attachment-focused EMDR. Highland Park https://www.highlandparktherapy.com/blog/2024/3/30/healing-att achment-trauma-through-attachment-focused-emdr#:~:text=Resear ch%20has%20shown%20promising%20results,functioning%20and% 20quality%20of%20life.

31. National Center for Biotechnology Information. (n.d.). Community interventions to promote mental health and well-being in individuals and communities. NCBI. Retrieved June 11, 2024, from https://w ww.ncbi.nlm.nih.gov/pmc/articles/PMC6440941/

32. Group Therapy Association. (n.d.). Adult attachment anxiety: Using group therapy to promote change. PubMed. Retrieved June 11, 2024, from https://pubmed.ncbi.nlm.nih.gov/24151103/

33. Fika Mental Health. (n.d.). *The Body Keeps the Score*. Retrieved from https://www.fikamentalhealth.com/post/the-body-keeps-the-score

www.ingramcontent.com/pod-product-compliance
Lightning Source LLC
Chambersburg PA
CBHW020409130626
46549CB00006B/2494